# The Old Made New: New Testament Application of Old Testament Stories

## Jeff Chitwood

Blauw Shack Media

Blauw Shack Media

ISBN: 979-8-9867313-8-4 (paperback)

Cover Art by Judy Chitwood

*Dedication*

I would like to dedicate this book to the congregation of Anchor Christian Church in Bonita Springs, Florida. Its contents were originally presented as a sermon series at Anchor. I received so much encouragement and support from the congregation that I decided to put the series into book format. Hopefully, more people will now be able to gain some insights and see how God works throughout the pages of scripture to bring about His purpose for mankind.

I would also like to make a special dedication to my wife, Judy. She has been an amazing wife, mother, and "minister's wife". I would not have had any success in the ministry had it not been for her continued support and encouragement.

# Table of Contents

## Foreword

When I first met Jeff over lunch, I saw a pastor with a heart for God, prayer, loving others, and sharing Jesus! Over the first six months that my wife and I attended Anchor Christian Church, it was clear that Jeff was a very humble individual, as was his wife, Judy. They both have a servant's heart for God's people! Jeff has since become a valuable friend, one that you will hopefully come to know through his book, *The Old Made New*.

Jeff has been a pastor for 46 years, ministering to God's children, wearing the many hats of a pastor; by God's grace, he still has a continued passion to grow closer to Christ and to grow God's people, as well as bring others to Christ! Christ gave His church gifts of pastors and teachers (Ephesians 4:11). As a teacher, Jeff has a gift for presenting God's Word in truth and love. His sermons are gospel-centered, led, and inspired by the Holy Spirit. He has a passion for teaching others about growing in Christ through the Bible, which includes the whole Bible, both the Old Testament and the New Testament. In today's world, many churches have broadened God's Word and consider the Old Testament irrelevant. So, it is exciting to be able to pick up a book that is based on Scriptural truths, using both the Old and New Testament as examples of walking in our everyday lives!

In this book, Jeff presents Bible stories that flow together in both the Old and New Testaments, and he compares and explains them. Then, he provides suggestions for your personal growth and understanding! He challenges you in your walk. Jeff puts the Bible in plain language and for a simple life application and makes it relevant to our lives today. As you read this book, hear Jeff's passion for God's Word. Listen to the challenges he presents to you, as the reader, to pursue God and become more like Jesus through His Word.

Someone once said that "the Old Testament and New Testament, with their distinct themes and messages, are like two movements in a symphony. Each has its unique tone and pace, but together they create a harmonious story of humanity's relationship with God." As you delve deeper into these differences, you will find yourself journeying into the heart of God's unfolding story, a story of love, redemption, and a need for transformation.

As we approach the last days, nothing is more important than growing in our understanding of the ways of God so that even when we find His plans unexpected or confusing, our hearts can be firmly established in the knowledge of His love, goodness, and trustworthiness. Whether you are a curious seeker, a new believer, or have been reading the Bible most of your life, this book is for you! No matter where you are in your spiritual journey, this book has something for you. Jeff has interwoven the Old Testament and the New Testament to bring it alive so that you know God intimately by growing a deep relationship with Him! As you read the passages that Jeff chose to combine, you suddenly start to feel challenged, "is part of me still living in my 'old self'?" That is not God's plan for you. Do not go into this book just to read a book for interest or knowledge, but be open to the Spirit's leading, convictions, and action.

This book might question you where you are in life. Have you put off the old self completely and put on the new with the Holy Spirit? This book will either convict you or confirm where you are. It is not optional. Each chapter will keep you on the edge of your seat, waiting to hear "the rest of the story," as Paul Harvey used to say. Jeff clearly shows you one of the messages of his book in Chapter 2 & Chapter 3: our need for salvation! I urge you, as you read these chapters and stories, to consider the significance of the old made new in your life.

In a rapidly changing culture, we need a return to sound biblical truth. We need something to help us step back, get a grip on the vast scope of the biblical truth from Genesis to Revelation, and let the truth of the major themes of the Bible guide our lives. This is what *The Old Made New* does for us. The insights in this book are wonderfully stimulating. As you read these pages, you will probably say several times, "I never realized that before!" The Bible changes lives! It is a lamp to show us God's way, and it is a sword that pierces deep into our hearts so we can experience God more fully than we ever imagined! *The Old Made New*, the accomplishment of combining the Old Testament and New Testament, would have been impossible if the two Books did not have a Divine Author!

I am delighted to endorse *The Old Made New* as a challenging and inspiring invitation to go deeper in intimacy with God through His Word! An intimacy that cannot help but challenge us to become more like Christ! May God use this book to call each of us to love others and share the good news of God's forgiveness, peace, and hope to a confused and dying world through Jesus Christ!

Rocky Zinser

## *Preface*

If you are like many people, you have heard and known some of the stories of the OT, like Creation, Adam and Eve, Noah's Ark, or Jonah in the belly of a whale. Those are great stories, and we have probably learned different lessons from them. Unfortunately, we don't think much beyond those lessons and rarely think about how the rest of the Bible looks at them.

As a minister, I am always trying to look ahead and think about the next sermon series I will be doing. While I was nearing the end of a series through the writings of John, I thought I would spend some time in the Old Testament. But the more I thought about that, God seemed to put on my heart, "If the people only know the Old Testament stories but don't find Jesus and the message of the New Testament in those stories, then they are missing out on the beauty and message of the whole Bible." That gave me the idea for the next sermon series and thus the content of this book: The Old Made New. We need to see how the Old Testament and the New Testament work together in tandem. They do not present two separate messages. They both focus on the ultimate message of the Bible - salvation. He wants His creation, you and me, to spend eternity with Him.

In my study of the "Old Made New," I found that the New Testament takes Old Testament stories and gives them a fresh meaning and application. The fresh meaning and application can be taken and applied to our daily lives. I want to make the Old Testament "new" again. That can be done by seeing that the Old Testament story is a vital part of understanding the New Testament story. Seeing how both of them present a message makes God's story relevant to our lives today.

I share many scripture passages in this book. I don't want to assume that everyone knows the stories well enough by just having a reference given. It is also important to know the passages well to get the full picture of how the Old Testament and New Testament work together.

I also want to give a special thanks to Roger VanderKolk for helping facilitate the development of this book and Ann Phillips for her expertise in editing and sharing insights.

### Applying the Word to Your Life Study Guide

I hope that you will use the Study Guide at the end of each chapter to help you and others go deeper in their walk with God. It is designed with a dual purpose: to guide a personal study as well as to give an outline for a group study. Each guide has four sections. The questions are not simply a "quiz" over the content of the chapter but rather a guide to help you go deeper into the Word. Each section aims to lead a study from simple reflection to life application. If you are using the guide to lead a small group study, I have explained the purpose of each section. This is meant to be a guide that can help you expand with your own questions and insights that connect with the group you are leading. At the beginning of each study you will see a line about prayer. I put this in intentionally because it is very important when studying God's Word.  Pray that He will direct your thoughts and heart.

**Focus Your Mind and Heart** – These questions are to engage the mind and heart in the study. They should help direct the focus on the theme of the chapter. You may have other questions that might spark interest. Let God guide your heart and focus your mind as you begin to see what He has to say to you.

**Examine the Word -** The point of the study is to see what God has to say. This section will ask you to go back and look at the scripture passages that were dealt with in the chapter. The focus of the study should be on the scripture, not simply what I say about the scriptures. By using a Concordance or Topical search online, you may find other scriptures that are relevant to the discussion.

**Take a Look at Your Life** – This section guides you to examine how the scripture relates to your life. Personal reflection is an important part of growing in the Lord. This is where God helps you "connect the dots" between His Word and your life.

**Apply It to Your Life** – If all we do is know the Word and reflect on the Word, without applying the Word, we have stopped short of what

God wants us to do. This final section is meant to give practical application suggestions to the Word as presented in the chapter. Please add to this section. Think about real and practical ways to apply the Word to life.

# CHAPTER ONE

## *Looking at the Old Testament & New Testament Together*

The Bible is one book but is also a collection of 66 books. It contains the consistent message of God to mankind. 2 Timothy 3:16 tells us that *"All Scripture is God-breathed and is useful for teaching, rebuking, correcting and training in righteousness."* From this verse, we can see that the words of the Bible came from God – "God-breathed" – and that it is good for guiding us through teaching, confrontation, correction, and training. In other words, it is not just a book to make us "feel good" but has the purpose of shaping and molding us into the person that God wants.

### The Structure

We know the Bible as one book, but it does have different parts. The two major parts are the Old Testament and the New Testament. The Old Testament contains 39 books written in Hebrew. Everything in the Old Testament contains stories and events that happened before Jesus came to the earth.

The New Testament contains 27 books written mainly in the 1st-century language of Koine Greek (the common spoken and written language of the early Roman empire). The New Testament tells the story of Jesus in the Gospels (Matthew, Mark, Luke, John), the history of how the church got started in the Book of Acts, and the rest is written to early Christians and specific churches to help them live their lives in a new faith called Christianity.

### The Author

The Bible has one author – God. God used 40 different men of diverse backgrounds over a period of 1500 years to record His message. He used a man named Moses, who was a shepherd by vocation but had been raised in the culture and royalty of Egypt. Another was Joshua, who was mentored by Moses but became a military leader and overseer of a nation in infancy. There were men from various backgrounds, like Isaiah, Jeremiah, and Ezra, who became prophets and were chosen to share the message of warning and encouragement to the people of Israel. In the New Testament, we have a Jewish man named Matthew, who worked as a tax collector for Rome. Luke, who was a physician, but used his gift of communication to write down an orderly account of all that he had seen and heard. We also have John, a fisherman and a common laborer among the people, and Paul, a religious leader who turned evangelist and supported himself as a tent maker. The above list is not all-inclusive, but it shows us that God used a variety of men from all walks of life to share His message throughout the ages.

It is amazing that over the course of time and through quite a diverse group of writers, God's message throughout the Bible is understandable and intentional and has a purpose. God wants His children, whom He created, to live a life on earth that will bring them to live in heaven with Him for eternity.

### Why Study the Old and New?

Why take the time to study the Bible—the Old and New Testaments together? The Bible records the past, speaks to the present, and projects the future. The Old and New Testaments work together to give mankind God's complete message. If we just study the New Testament without knowing the background that comes from the Old Testament, then there are many gaps in the New Testament message.

Jesus wants His followers to understand the Old Testament writings. When appearing to the disciples after His resurrection, He said this to them: *"This is what I told you while I was still with you: Everything must be fulfilled that is written about me in the Law of Moses, the Prophets, and the Psalms. Then he opened their minds so they could understand the Scriptures" (Luke 24:44,45).* We sometimes forget that the Bible for the New Testament Christians was the Old Testament scriptures. The Old Testament presents the story of the work of God in the lives of His people before Jesus, but it is an incomplete story. The Old Testament story finds completion in the New Testament story. Yet, just as the New Testament story completes the Old Testament, it also points to a future that has yet to be fulfilled. So, for us to be a part of God's story, we need to understand God's story - the Old and New Testament. Let's begin that journey together.

## Study Guide: Looking at the Old Testament and New Testament Together

Pray for God's guidance and insight as you study His Word. He knows your heart and what you need to learn.

### Focus Your Mind and Heart

Take some time and reflect on the Bible and what it has meant to your life. Be honest, be real.

- Why do some see the Bible just as a book of "neat" stories?
- What are some reasons that you or others don't always turn to God's Word first?
- How is the Bible relevant to your life today?
- How will you let God change your heart and mind through the study of His Word?
- What are some questions that you would add to the ones above?

### Examine the Word

2 Timothy 3:16 tells us that *"All Scripture is God-breathed and is useful for teaching, rebuking, correcting and training in righteousness."*

The above verse is a powerful verse. What is meant by the following phrases? Give some examples of what you mean.

- All Scripture –
- God Breathed –
- Useful for teaching –
- Useful for rebuking –
- Useful for correcting –
- Useful for training in righteousness –

Pop Quiz – On a separate piece of paper write out as many of the books of the Bible you can remember and try to put them in the proper order. Old Testament first, then the New Testament.

How did you do?

Why is it helpful to know what the books of the Bible are?

Have you ever wondered about how the people in the day of Jesus interpreted and applied the Old Testament stories to their life? Can you think of any examples in the New Testament where an Old Testament story was used to make a life application lesson?

Observations you made when thinking about the Bible:

**Take a Look at Your Life**

The message of the Bible is consistent from the beginning to the end. Why is that important to you?

If the Bible was full of contradictions and inconsistencies, what would that do to your opinion about the Bible?

How much time do you spend in the Word of God each week?

**Apply it to Your Life**

List three things you can do to make the Word of God more real in your life.

     1 –

     2 –

     3 –

Set a goal of increasing the time you spend in the word each day. Find a consistent time and place that works for your schedule.

What are some areas that you "waste time" in that could be converted to time in the Word?

# CHAPTER TWO

## *A New Beginning*

### Genesis 1 and John 1

A New Beginning Starts with God

The opening words of the Bible are foundational to the rest of God's story. Genesis 1:1 says, *"In the beginning God created the heavens and the earth"*. Accepting the Bible's first verse is foundational to understanding the rest of the Bible. It all begins with God, who created us and gives us an opportunity to write our life story. I pray that we will all write a story that is pleasing to God.

When it comes to God's story, it is amazing how much time, effort, and money man has expended explaining the beginning of the universe – the origins of mankind – the galaxies – geology – science, and DNA. Mankind looks everywhere except in the first verse of the Bible. Believing that this thing we call "life" did not happen by mistake but had a creator and design behind it is basic to finding purpose in life.

A new beginning for you may mean looking back at the beginning and discovering that God is the one thing you may have been missing. The story that begins in Genesis 1 is carried throughout the Old Testament, and it is picked up and continued in the New Testament. It continues in the Gospel of John.

A New Beginning Continues with Jesus

*"In the beginning was the Word, and the Word was with God, and the Word was God. He was with God in the beginning. Through him all things were made; without him nothing was made that has been made. In him was life, and that life was the light of all mankind" (John 1:1-4).*

It is interesting to compare John 1 with Genesis 1. In Genesis 1 we find these words: *"In the beginning God created the heavens and the earth . . . and God said, 'Let there be light' and there was light. . . and the Spirit of God was hovering over the waters" (Genesis 1:1-3).* In creation, we have a picture of the Trinity – God, Jesus, and the Holy Spirit. God created in Genesis 1:1. In Genesis 1:2, *"the Spirit of God was hovering over the waters."* In John 1:2, Jesus *"was with God in the beginning."* This is key in seeing the flow of the message of the Bible: Jesus was there with God in the beginning, the creation of the heavens and the earth. Just as light was created in the beginning for the world, Jesus came to the earth as the light for all mankind - *"In him was life, and that life was the light of men" (John 1: 4).* In Christ, we have the creator of the world come to this earth so that we could fully grasp the intent of His creation. But the story doesn't end there. We need to see what it means to be a part of the new creation.

## A New Beginning Depends on You

"So from now on we regard no one from a worldly point of view. Though we once regarded Christ in this way, we do so no longer" (2 Corinthians 5:16).

Paul is saying that Jesus' coming to earth changed everything. While Jesus was on earth, people viewed Him as a man and did not fully grasp who He was. But the resurrection changed all of that. Mankind came to see that He was fully God and fully man. Coming to terms with that changes everything. That is why Paul goes on to say in the very next verse: *"Therefore, if anyone is in Christ, the new creation has come: The old has gone, the new is here" (2 Corinthians 5:17)!*

God's creation finds completion when we let Him create a "new" person in us. New from the inside out. Paul had two different words to choose from when he used our English word "new." One of the words meant "new" as on a timeline – today is a "new" day on the calendar. The other word meant "new" in quality – today is a "new" day because I have a fresh start in life. Guess which word Paul uses here? Right – the second one. All things are made "new" when you come to Christ. When you accept that He is the creator of the world and the light of the world, it all comes together. The "old" is made "new" through Jesus.

## How Will Your Beginning End?

I read about a character in a book once who had an interesting dream. The character dreamed that she was standing in line with a bunch of people, going up a staircase to face God. All the people had notebooks in their hands, and they were frantically flipping through the pages of those notebooks. She looked down at her book and noticed that the last several pages were blank. It hit her that her story was not finished. She wanted to finish her story. So, she raised her hand and said, "Sir, as I read my story, I am pretty sure you are not going to be pleased with it. May I go back and fill in these blank pages and finish my story? Finish it in a way that you will be pleased with. God smiled and said, "Yes."

What's your story? What do your past, present, and future look like? As I reflect on my life, I look back at forty-six years of ministry. Over those years, there have been some mountaintop experiences and some journeys through the valley. But each one of those experiences has helped me write my story. Have there been things I would do differently? Yes. Are there things that I would not change a bit? Yes. The older I get, the more I realize that each day I am writing a new page in my story. My prayer is that God will help me write each page in the future. My prayer is that I "finish well."

Do you have anything "old" that needs to be made "new" again in your life? You can only make the "old" "new" when you let God and Jesus be a part of your story. Take a look at your past and see what God can do with it. You might be surprised at what He wants to do with your future!

## Study Guide: A New Beginning

Pray for God's guidance and insight as you study His Word. He knows your heart and what you need to learn.

### Focus Your Mind and Heart

When was the last time you got something brand new? What was special about that?

What does it take to take something "old" and make it "new" again?

Who are some of the people in the Bible that got a "new chance at life?"

What kind of questions would you ask someone if they told you they felt like a "new" person?

### Examine the Word

*"In the beginning God created the heavens and the earth." (Genesis 1:1)*

*"In the beginning was the Word, and the Word was with God, and the Word was God. He was with God in the beginning. Through him all things were made; without him nothing was made that has been made. In him was life, and that life was the light of all mankind" (John 1:1-4).*

Those two passages above are powerful passages about God and His creative power. What are some of God's attributes that can be seen when pondering the meaning of these passages?

*"So from now on we regard no one from a worldly point of view. Though we once regarded Christ in this way, we do so no longer" (2 Corinthians 5:16).*

What does the above verse say about how we should view others who come to Christ?

How should we view those who have yet to come to Christ?

Paul goes on in 2 Corinthians to say this: *"Therefore, if anyone is in Christ, he is a new creation; the old has gone, the new has come!" (2 Corinthians 5:17).*

How does the explanation of the two words for "new" in the "A New Beginning Depends on You" section in this chapter impact your understanding of verse 17 and someone who is "new" in Christ?

### Take a Look at Your Life

Describe a time when you felt you lost the "newness" in your relationship with Christ. What are some things that caused that to happen?

What are some things that help you keep your "newness" in your relationship with Christ?

### Apply it to Your Life

Do you have anything "old" that needs to be made "new" again in your life? What are some of those things?

What can you do this week to be renewed?

Write out a prayer asking God for His help in this area of your life:

# CHAPTER THREE

## *From Mess to Messiah*

### Genesis 2 & Romans 5

Have you ever had one of those really good days where everything just seemed to go right? You get up in the morning, and you feel good. You had a good night's sleep. You step on the scale, and you lost five pounds overnight! You have your favorite food for breakfast, whatever that is – my guess is that it could be anything from steak and eggs to a giant donut from your favorite donut shop! You get in your car to go somewhere; it could be work, it could be the store, and there is hardly any traffic. You hit every stop light green, and life is going smoothly.

Then, all of a sudden, it happens. You have a tire blow out, you swerve off the road, go down a ditch and your car scraps a big tree all the way down the passenger side. Suddenly, your good day isn't so good anymore. Suddenly, the day is a mess. The next several hours are going to be a struggle to recover from everything that just happened. But by the end of the day, you get your car out of the ditch, your insurance says they have you covered, and you realize that God watched over you. You are thankful you were not injured. The mess of the accident got cleaned up, and you know that life is good.

How realistic is that scenario? It is not out of the realm of possibility (except for the part about losing 5 lbs. overnight!). Have you ever wondered what could turn a good day into a bad day in the Bible? Then what can take that bad day and make it good again? I want to share a condensed version of the story found in Genesis 1, 2 & 3 and see how things got messy.

Things Got Messy Early On

It doesn't take long into the story of man to see that man soon made a mess of things. The best way to tell the story is to simply read it for yourself.

*"Then God looked over all he had made, and he saw that it was very good! And evening passed and morning came, marking the sixth day. So the creation of the heavens and the earth and everything in them was completed. On the seventh day God had finished his work of creation, so he rested from all his work"* (Genesis 1:31-2:2, NLT).

It was a good day. Creation is complete, everything is good, and God takes a day off. If the story ended there, it would present a nice finished picture. But the story didn't end there; it continued.

*"The Lord God formed the man from the dust of the ground and breathed into his nostrils the breath of life, and the man became a living being"* (Genesis 2:7).

*"The Lord God took the man and put him in the Garden of Eden to work it and take care of it. And the Lord God commanded the man, 'You are free to eat from any tree in the garden; but you must not eat from the tree of the knowledge of good and evil, for when you eat of it you will surely die.' The Lord God said, 'It is not good for the man to be alone. I will make a helper suitable for him'"* (Genesis 2:15-18).

The one thing that was not good was that man was alone. There is a show on Netflix called *Alone*. The show is about ten people who are flown out into the wilderness with some basic survival gear. They are isolated from everyone. They are completely alone. The show's winner is the one who can survive in the wilderness the longest in total isolation. The longest survivor so far in the show stayed in the wilderness for 100 days.

What is the one thing that almost all contestants struggle with the most, other than the lack of food? Being alone. They miss their family and friends. Why is that? Because God created a need in us for companionship.

Even though Adam had everything he needed for survival, he was alone. God had a way to take care of that loneliness: create Eve. When Eve entered the picture, things changed for the better – at least for a while. The opening words of Genesis 3 are like watching a movie. The scene opens, and the music changes, and we hear the low, evil sound: "Da, da, da, dah!"

*"Now the serpent was more crafty than any of the wild animals the Lord God had made. He said to the woman, 'Did God really say, You must not eat from any tree in the garden?' The woman said to the serpent, 'We may eat fruit from the trees in the garden, but God did say, You must not eat fruit from the tree that is in the middle of the garden, and you must not touch it, or you will die'" (Genesis 3:1-3).*

Now, it seems that Eve understood God's guidelines for life. She didn't hesitate to answer the serpent's question. She didn't try to think of a good answer to impress Satan. She simply stated what God told her. I don't know how she could have stated it any clearer: *"But God did say."* Satan's motives were clear, though. He wanted to turn what was good into bad.

*"'You will not surely die,' the serpent said to the woman. 'For God knows that when you eat of it your eyes will be opened, and you will be like God, knowing good and evil.' When the woman saw that the fruit of the tree was good for food and pleasing to the eye, and also desirable for gaining wisdom, she took some and ate it. She also gave some to her husband, who was with her, and he ate it. Then the eyes of both of them were opened, and they realized they were naked; so they sewed fig leaves together and made coverings for themselves" (Genesis 3:4-7).*

All of a sudden, a good day becomes a bad day. When you know the rules and deliberately break them, it eventually catches up with you. That is what happened with Adam and Eve.

*"Then the man and his wife heard the sound of the Lord God as he was walking in the garden in the cool of the day, and they hid from the Lord God among the trees of the garden. But the Lord God called to the man, 'Where are you?' He answered, 'I heard you in the garden, and I was afraid because I was naked; so I hid.' And he said, 'Who told you that you were naked? Have you eaten from the tree that I commanded you not to eat from?' The man said, 'The woman you put here with me — she gave me some fruit from the tree, and I ate it.' Then the Lord God said to the woman, 'What is this you have done?' The woman said, 'The serpent deceived me, and I ate.' So the Lord God said to the serpent, 'Because you have done this, Cursed are you above all the livestock and all the wild animals! You will crawl on your belly and you will eat dust all the days of your life. And I will put hostility between you and the woman, and between your offspring and hers; he*

*will crush your head, and you will strike his heel'" (Genesis 3:8-14).*

*"To Adam he said, 'Because you listened to your wife and ate from the tree about which I commanded you, You must not eat of it, Cursed is the ground because of you; through painful toil you will eat of it all the days of your life. It will produce thorns and thistles for you, and you will eat the plants of the field. By the sweat of your brow you will eat your food until you return to the ground, since from it you were taken; for dust you are and to dust you will return" (Genesis 3:17-19).*

*"After he drove the man out, he placed on the east side of the Garden of Eden cherubim and a flaming sword flashing back and forth to guard the way to the tree of life" (Gen 3:24).*

That wasn't a good day for Adam and Eve or for the future of mankind. Suddenly, everything had changed. They had pretty much made a mess of things. This mess is commonly referred to as the "fall of man." When man moved from a perfect existence and a perfect relationship with God to a messed-up existence and a broken relationship, it was a sad day. What happened that day had implications for generations and generations to come. The disobedience of Adam and Eve is marked as the beginning of what we now call "sin." The sin that entered the world that day had two major impacts.

## The Mess Broke a Perfect Relationship Between God and Man

In the beginning, God took care of all Adam and Eve's needs. They had everything. God would speak to Adam, and Adam would freely speak back. God saw a void in Adam's completeness, and He completed that void by creating Eve. Everything was good until Satan introduced doubt, and doubt turned to rationalization, and rationalization turned into sin.

It was a good day before Adam and Eve made the mess. They were not ashamed of anything and walked freely in the garden. After making the mess—sinning—they tried to hide themselves from God. That separation created a vast gulf between God and man.

<u>The Mess Brought Pain and Evil into the World</u>

I've been asked, and you have probably asked it: "Why does God allow pain and suffering in the world? Why do bad things happen to good people?" I don't have all the answers to those questions, but here is what I do know.

The sin of Adam and Eve opened the door to a multitude of bad things in this world. Things like pain and suffering and loneliness and despair and confusion and death. It shows us how Satan can take over the hearts and minds of people and cause them to do bad things – make bad decisions – and let their hearts be guided by evil rather than good.

The lies of Satan fooled Eve, and it has been happening to mankind ever since. He has not rested one day from destroying the lives of people since that day in the garden. We live in a broken world because of the sin in the Garden of Eden. Pain, suffering, and evil entered the world because of the sin in the garden.

The mess that was made then will not be made completely right until the words of Revelation are fulfilled: *"He will wipe every tear from their eyes. There will be no more death or mourning or crying or pain, for the old order of things has passed away. He who was seated on the throne said, 'I am making everything new!' Then he said, 'Write this down, for these words are trustworthy and true'"* (Rev 21:4-5).

The sin in the garden not only impacted the heart of men, but it impacted the very Creation itself. God says to Adam: *"Cursed is the ground because of you; through painful toil you will eat of it all the days of your life. It will produce thorns and thistles for you"* (Genesis 3:17b,18). There are earthquakes and tornadoes and hurricanes and drought and floods. Creation itself is not what it was in the beginning. Paul says in Romans 8:22, *"We know that the whole creation has been groaning as in the pains of childbirth right up to the present time."*

So, what started out as a good day in the Garden of Eden turned into a bad day, and we have been living with the effects of that bad day for a very long time. What is it going to take to make it a good day?

<u>God Cleans Up the Mess by Promising a Messiah</u>

After the sin in the garden, God addressed Satan, and He makes this statement in Genesis 3:15: *"And I will cause hostility between you and* the woman, and between your offspring and her offspring. He will strike your head, and you will strike his heel" (NLT).

That last phrase, "he will crush your head, and you will strike his heel," is the first promise in the Bible of what it will take to make a bad day and a good day. Those words are the promise of a Messiah, a deliverer. Jesus would come and "crush" the head of Satan through the resurrection – victory over death. Satan would inflict a "bruise" on the heel of Jesus - He would suffer the pain of death on the cross. Which would you rather have, a crushed head or a bruised heel? I've had a bruised heel, and it hurts, but I would much rather have that than a crushed head. What that graphically illustrates is the victory of Jesus over the power of Satan.

This is where the "Old Made New" comes in. The events that began in Genesis find their completion in the New Testament story. Let's look at two New Testament passages that show the consistency of God's message and plan for mankind from the beginning to the end.

The Messiah Cleans Up the Mess

Have you ever made a mess and then had to clean it up? Most guys are thinking – I don't think so. Their wives would disagree. There is a passage in Romans that directly links the events in the Garden of Eden to Jesus: ". . . death reigned from the time of Adam to the time of Moses, even over those who did not sin by breaking a command, as did Adam, who was a pattern of the one to come. But the gift is not like the trespass. For if the many died by the trespass of the one man, how much more did God's grace and the gift that came by the grace of the one man, Jesus Christ, overflow to the many! . . . For if, by the trespass of the one man, death reigned through that one man, how much more will those who receive God's abundant provision of grace and of the gift of righteousness reign in life through the one man, Jesus Christ" (Romans 5:14-17). Paul then sums it up in one simple statement in 1 Corinthians 15:22: "For as in Adam all die, so in Christ all will be made alive."

This is an amazing passage that shows how God took the mess created in the Garden of Eden and cleaned it up through Jesus' life, death, and resurrection. What does this have to do with you?

The Messiah wants to Help Clean Up Your Mess

If your first thought was, "What mess?" when you read the above section title, you need to think again. The sin that was introduced in the Garden of Eden continues in your life and my life today. You might be thinking, "Wait a minute, I didn't eat the fruit. That is all on Eve!" But just as that sin of disobedience in the Garden broke the relationship between Adam and Eve and God, sin today does the same thing to our relationship with God.

The good news is that Jesus takes away our sins. We can't do it ourselves. Sins are forgiven through the sacrifice of Jesus on the cross. The effects of sin and death were defeated through the resurrection. The great news is that Jesus invites us to come and receive what He freely offers. Revelation 22:12-15 gives a beautiful promise: *"Look, I am coming soon, bringing my reward with me to repay all people according to their deeds. I am the Alpha and the Omega, the First and the Last, the Beginning and the End. Blessed are those who wash their robes. They will be permitted to enter through the gates of the city and eat the fruit from the tree of life."*

Everyone is invited to eat the fruit from the Tree of Life—what a turnaround from what we find in Genesis. What was forbidden in Genesis 3 is now open to all who accept the promised one, Jesus Christ. The one who is prophesied in the first book of the Bible comes to crush the head of Satan once and for all in the closing chapter of the Bible.

From beginning to end, the message is the same. When we make a mess of things, God sends a Messiah to clean up the mess. He takes the dirt and filth and chaos of the mess and makes all things new again. The events in the first few chapters of the Bible set a different tone. Instead of hiding in the garden, hoping that God will not find us, the final chapter of the Bible declares these words for you and me today: *"The Spirit and the bride say, 'Come.' Let anyone who hears this say, 'Come.' Let anyone who is thirsty come. Let anyone who desires drink freely from the water of life"* (Revelation 22:17).

Are things a little messy in your life? Let Him help clean up the mess.

## Study Guide: From Mess to Messiah

Pray for God's guidance and insight as you study His Word. He knows your heart and what you need to learn.

### Focus Your Mind and Heart

Chapter 3 opens with a scenario of a good day turned bad. Describe a time that you had a day like that.

What are some of the factors that make a "good day" or a "bad day"?

What do you think about the current state of the world? Is it a "mess" that needs a "Messiah"? Why?

### Examine the Word

God gave Adam a lot of freedom in the Garden of Eden. What was the one restriction He gave? What purpose do God's laws or commandments serve?

Look at Genesis 3:1-7. Identify all the deceptive phrases Satan used on Eve. What are some deceptive phrases that Satan uses today?

When God confronted Adam and Eve about what they had done (Genesis 3:8-14), they played the "blame game." Why do you think they did that?

What is the significance of Genesis 3:15 in God's plan for mankind?

How do Romans 5:14-17 and 1 Corinthians 15:22 show the flow of God's plan of salvation for mankind from the Old Testament to the New Testament?

### Take a Look at Your Life

Describe a time when Satan tried to deceive you into believing a lie.

Have you ever played the "blame game" like Adam and Eve did? How did that work out for you?

What would you share with someone who says, "My life is a mess and I need some help"?

**Apply it to Your Life**

Think about the "messes" God has cleaned up in your life. Spend some time in prayer thanking Him for what He has done in your life.

Do you still have some "messes" that need to be cleaned up? Apply this verse: Hebrew 4:16 – *"Let us then approach the throne of grace with confidence, so that we may receive mercy and find grace to help us in our time of need."*

# CHAPTER FOUR

## *"Am I My Brother's Keeper?" - Jesus Answers Cain*

**Genesis 4:2-26, Hebrews 11:4; 1 John 3:11-18**

As a father of two daughters, I played a number of games with them over the years. One phrase that you could count on during some of those games was, "That's not fair!" It inevitably came out when one seemed to get an advantage over the other. My classic comeback when I heard that was, "Life's not fair." Maybe you have even said that once or twice in your life. The phrase or idea is not new. It has been around for a long time. A very long time. The exact words are not used, but they are implied all the way back in chapter 4 of the book of Genesis.

As we take this journey of making the "old" "new," it is important to see how the Old Testament stories were used in the New Testament. In making that comparison, we must also see how they are relevant to our lives today. So, let's see where it all started.

<u>The Story of Cain</u>

*"When they grew up, Abel became a shepherd, while Cain cultivated the ground. When it was time for the harvest, Cain presented some of his crops as a gift to the Lord. Abel also brought a gift—the best of the firstborn lambs from his flock. The Lord accepted Abel and his gift, but he did not accept Cain and his gift. This made Cain very angry, and he looked dejected" (Genesis 4:2-5, NLT).*

Upon the first reading of this story, it is easy to say, "That doesn't sound fair! They both offered a gift." But if you look closely at how the gifts are described, I think you will see the difference. Cain presented "some" of his crop. Abel presented "the best of the firstborn lambs." There is a big difference between "some" and "the best." That difference was the key to what happened next. *"'Why are you so angry?' the Lord asked Cain. 'Why do you look so dejected? You will be accepted if you do what is right. But if you refuse to do what is right, then watch out! Sin is crouching at the door, eager to control you. But you must subdue it and be its master'" (Genesis 4:6-7, NLT).*

After the statement in verse seven, some time passes. We don't know how much time, but Cain did not let his anger go. He had a decision to make. Was he going to do what was right – subdue his anger or refuse to subdue it and let his anger control him? We find out as the story continues: *"One day Cain suggested to his brother, 'Let's go out into the fields.' And while they were in the field, Cain attacked his brother, Abel, and killed him" (Genesis 4:8, NLT).*

What did Cain do with his anger? He let it take over his heart and life. What was the result? *"Afterward the Lord asked Cain, 'Where is your brother? Where is Abel?' 'I don't know,' Cain responded. 'Am I my brother's keeper?'" (Genesis 4:9, NLT).*

Cain's response was not one of his finer moments. He chose to lie to God and have a haughty attitude toward Him. The question he asked has become a well-known question over the centuries— "Am I my brother's Keeper?" The question has morphed into a response that causes people today to use it to deflect the responsibility of caring for others.

The story of Cain and Abel is a tragic one. It has been told over and over again throughout history. It is a story of jealousy, anger, revenge and murder. All the things you need for a crime thriller novel or movie for today. But their story is not a story of fiction. It is a story that did not escape the New Testament story. It is referred to twice in the New Testament, and in both instances, there is a great lesson for us to learn.

So, are you your brother's keeper? Considering what the New Testament teaches, I would say, "Yes, you are your brother's keeper, and He is watching to see what you will do."

## When it Comes to Dealing with Your Brother - Let Your Brother See Your Faith

This is the first reference to the story of Cain and Abel in the New Testament, found in Hebrews 11. The writer of Hebrews emphasizes Abel: *"It was by faith that Abel brought a more acceptable offering to God than Cain did. Abel's offering gave evidence that he was a righteous man, and God showed his approval of his gifts. Although Abel is long dead, he still speaks to us by his example of faith" (Hebrews 11:4).*

Hebrews chapter 11 is known as the "Hall of Fame of Faith". It is no surprise to find names like Noah, Abraham, Isaac, Jacob, Moses, and David. But the story of Cain and Abel? Their names are the first ones mentioned in the "Hall of Fame" chapter. The lesson in faith comes from seeing the contrast between Cain and Abel.

It is noted that Abel was a "righteous" man. He was a man who lived by the right choices. Abel's faith in God compelled him to give the best he had. He didn't give what was left over. He didn't give just a token. He gave his best.

Giving your best to God is evidence of faith. It shows that you put your trust in Him and that you want to honor Him. Faithfulness is seen in the decisions you make when deciding between right and wrong. Remember what God said to Cain: *"You will be accepted if you do what is right. But if you refuse to do what is right, then watch out! Sin is crouching at the door, eager to control you" (Gen 4:7).*

Faithfulness is seen in how you handle tough times in life, how you respond when someone wrongs you, and how you treat other people. The writer of Hebrews reminds us that, yes, we are our brother's keeper when it comes to life. Our lives should exemplify what it means to be faithful to God so that our brothers can learn from our example.

The story of Cain and Abel is mentioned one other time in the New Testament. The second time, the emphasis is on Cain.

## When it Comes to Dealing with Your Brother - Let Your Brother See Your Love

Jesus doesn't address the story of Cain and Abel in the gospels, but John takes the words of Jesus and says this: *"This is the message you have heard from the beginning: We should love one another" (1 John 3:11).* Jesus laid it out to His disciples – Guys, the people will know you are my disciples if you love one another. John knew how important it was for the people of the church to live out the words and teachings of Jesus when it came to love.

If people were to come to this new faith, they had to see that it was real, and they would see its reality demonstrated in how they loved one another. John uses Cain to warn us what to watch out for: *"We must not be like Cain, who belonged to the evil one and killed his brother. And why did he kill him? Because Cain had been doing what was evil, and his brother had been doing what was righteous" (1 John 3:12, NLT).*

Notice the interesting phrase – "had been doing" – applied to both of them. Cain – what had he been doing? "Evil". Abel – what had he been doing? "What was righteous." Here is what struck me about the phrase "had been doing". The phrase does not imply just one act but rather a pattern of activity. The attitudes and actions of the heart in both of them had been demonstrated time and time again. Cain didn't just have a bad day; it went deeper than that.

The New Testament interpretation seems to be that God's judgment on Cain and Abel resulted from their lives leading up to the sacrifice. What was the difference? Cain belonged to "the evil one" and had been doing what the evil one wanted him to do. Abel seemed to be doing the opposite.

Guess what? Things haven't changed that much over thousands of years! We still have a choice in how we are going to respond to the ideas and temptations that Satan puts in our way. We still have a choice whether we love as Jesus loved or not. John goes on to explain this and makes a practical application about this when it comes to our brothers – are we our brother's keepers? Listen to how John answers that: *"So don't be surprised, dear brothers and sisters, if the world hates you. If we love our Christian brothers and sisters, it proves that we have passed from death to life. But a person who has no love is still dead. Anyone who hates another brother or sister is really a murderer at heart. And you know that murderers don't have eternal life within them"* (1 John 3:13-15, NLT).

The most effective love your brother will know is what he sees. What does that type of love look like? Real love is a sacrifice: *"We know what real love is because Jesus gave up his life for us. So we also ought to give up our lives for our brothers and sisters"* (1 John 3:16, NLT). Jesus gave it all. We need to give it our all. Real love is seen in practical deeds: *"If someone has enough money to live well and sees a brother or sister in need but shows no compassion—how can God's love be in that person?"* (1 John 3:17, NLT). Real love shows the truth through actions: *"Dear children, let's not merely say that we love each other; let us show the truth by our actions"* (1 John 3:18, NLT).

Yes, we are our brother's keeper and we can learn a lot from two brothers that didn't get along very well.

We need to live a life of faith that can be seen every day of our lives.

We need to live a life of love that can be experienced by others.

**Study Guide: "Am I My Brother's Keeper?" Jesus Gives an Answer**

Pray for God's guidance and insight as you study His Word. He knows your heart and what you need to learn.

**Focus Your Mind and Heart**

Have you ever heard someone say, "That's not fair!" What usually prompts someone to say that?

Can you think of any stories in the Bible where the "That's not fair" line could have been used?

Are we responsible for the actions of others?

**Examine the Word**

Genesis 4:2-5 shows the difference between Cain and Abel. What do you think is the difference between "some" and "the best"?

What type of sin do you think was "crouching at Cain's door" in Genesis 4:6-7?

What emotions do you think Cain was experiencing when he said, *"Am I my brother's keeper?"* in Genesis 4:9?

How did Abel's offering give evidence that he was a righteous man? (Hebrews 11:4)

**Take a Look at Your Life**

Have you ever found yourself saying, "That's not fair!"? How did you deal with it?

Giving your best to God is evidence of faith. What impact does "giving your best" have on others?

**Apply it to Your Life**

When it comes to dealing with your brother – let your brother see your faith. List some practical ways you can let your brother see your faith.

When it comes to dealing with your brother – let your brother see your love. List some ways you can let your brother see your love.

# CHAPTER FIVE

*Noah and Us - We are in the Same Boat!*

**Genesis 6-9; Matthew 24:37-39; 1 Peter 3:18-21**

The story of Noah's Ark is one of the Bible's well-known stories. You have probably heard different lessons or sermons covering all kinds of different aspects of the story. However, since this book, *The Old Made New*, focuses on a specific area, we are not so concerned about all the possible applications that people have made concerning Noah. Instead, I believe it is more important to see how God applies the story to our lives. The New Testament refers to the story of Noah's Ark several different times.

First, let's revisit the story. Genesis 6-9 contains the entire story, but we will read just a few highlights from the story.

## The Story of Noah

*"The Lord observed the extent of human wickedness on the earth, and he saw that everything they thought or imagined was consistently and totally evil. So the Lord was sorry he had ever made them and put them on the earth. It broke his heart. And the Lord said, 'I will wipe this human race I have created from the face of the earth. Yes, and I will destroy every living thing—all the people, the large animals, the small animals that scurry along the ground, and even the birds of the sky. I am sorry I ever made them.' But Noah found favor with the Lord"* (Genesis 6:5-8, NLT).

Things must have been pretty bad on the earth for God to be sorry that He had ever made man. It looked like a lost cause until God came upon Noah. He stood out from all the people on the earth. He walked with God and had a relationship with Him. One day, God spoke to him and gave him some instructions.

*"Build a large boat from cypress wood and waterproof it with tar, inside and out. Then construct decks and stalls throughout its interior. Make the boat 450 feet long, 75 feet wide, and 45 feet high. Leave an 18-inch opening below the roof all*

*the way around the boat. Put the door on the side, and build three decks inside the boat—lower, middle, and upper. Look! I am about to cover the earth with a flood that will destroy every living thing that breathes. Everything on earth will die. But I will confirm my covenant with you. So enter the boat—you and your wife and your sons and their wives. Bring a pair of every kind of animal—a male and a female—into the boat with you to keep them alive during the flood" (Genesis 6:14-19, NLT).*

*"So Noah did everything exactly as God had commanded him" (Genesis 6:22, NLT).*

*"When everything was ready, the Lord said to Noah, 'Go into the boat with all your family, for among all the people of the earth, I can see that you alone are righteous'" (Genesis 7:1-2, NLT).*

Then it rained forty days and forty nights, and the earth opened up, and great springs of water came up out of the ground. After forty days the water stayed on the earth for another one hundred and fifty days.

There is a lot of information and different ideas you could focus on when it comes to the story of Noah's Ark. We will look at a couple of interesting things, but mainly, we are going to focus on the application of the story of Noah in the New Testament.

### Some Interesting Background on the Story of Noah

The ark itself was a very large boat. A couple of years ago we visited the "Ark Encounter" in Williamstown, KY. As you are nearing the ark on the highway, you are overwhelmed by its size. It was built to the dimensions given in Genesis: 450 feet long, 75 feet wide, and 45 feet high. If you were to stand it on end, it would be comparable to the Statue of Liberty stacked on top of itself 3.3 times. You could also compare it to the height of the Washington Monument.

A boat that big meant that there was a lot of space on board. Was it big enough to hold all the animals, provisions, tools, etc.? A lot of ink has been spilled over the ages arguing this point, but without going into all the formulas, yes, it was big enough to hold everything.

## Some Assumptions about the Story of Noah

1.  Assumption 1- It took 120 years to build the ark. I always grew up hearing that it took 120 years to build the Ark. Actually, Genesis never really says how long it took. The idea of the 120 years comes from Genesis 6:3: *"Then the Lord said, 'My Spirit will not contend with man forever, for he is mortal; his days will be a hundred and twenty years.'"* However, no time frame is given for how long after God made that statement that He told Noah to build the ark. The scholars from the Ark Encounter project say that it would have taken around 75 years to build the Ark.

2.  Assumption 2 - Noah preached to all the people and warned them about what was to come. Genesis does not mention Noah preaching to the people and warning them about anything. Noah is referred to as a *"preacher of righteousness"* in 2 Peter 2:5, but that is the only reference to something like that. It can be assumed that people asked some questions when they saw what he was doing, so those around him very well could have heard Noah's testimony about what God had asked him to do.

3.  Assumption 3 - They have found Noah's Ark in a mountain range in Turkey or Iran. Several documentaries have claimed to have found Noah's Ark, but they do not have any pictures for proof. In 2021, there was a find on the Turkey and Iran border that seemed to be remnants of a large boat 555 feet long, but it can't be confirmed that this is the ark. The bottom line is that we don't know, and you shouldn't base your faith on whether they found it or not.

The New Testament doesn't debate any of the above ideas, but they are interesting to consider. What we do know is that the story of Noah's Ark was well known in the days of the New Testament and is referred to six different times (Matthew 24:37.38; Luke 3:36; Luke 17:26,27; Hebrews 11:7; 1 Peter 3:30; 2 Peter 2:5). We are going to look at two of those occurrences.

Maybe you've heard the phrase – "We're all in the same boat." The phrase basically means that we are saying that we share the same circumstances or challenges. It could mean that we are in a mess together. I think that applies to the story of Noah. I want to share two applications of the story of Noah from the New Testament that show we are in the same boat as Noah. We share some of the same issues. The first is this:

## We are in the Same Boat Because the Heart of Man has Not Changed

The first reference to the story of Noah in the New Testament is in the context of Jesus teaching about His return and the end of time here on earth. It is about the end times. Listen to how Jesus applied it: *"When the Son of Man returns, it will be like it was in Noah's day. In those days before the flood, the people were enjoying banquets and parties and weddings right up to the time Noah entered his boat. People didn't realize what was going to happen until the flood came and swept them all away. That is the way it will be when the Son of Man comes"* (Matthew 24:37-39, NLT).

A lot of people talk about or ask, "What is it going to be like when Jesus returns?" Jesus answers the question for us – we don't have to guess - *"It will be like it was in Noah's day"*. That should spark this question – "What was it like in the Days of Noah?" Let me refresh your memory from a passage we looked at earlier: *"The Lord observed the extent of human wickedness on the earth, and he saw that everything they thought or imagined was consistently and totally evil. So the Lord was sorry he had ever made them and put them on the earth. It broke his heart"* (Genesis 6:5-6, NLT).

That says a lot about man and a lot about God. Regarding man: *"Everything they thought or imagined was consistently and totally evil."* Regarding God – *"It broke His heart."* Jesus addresses the people's mindset of that day in Matthew 24:38,39 when He says, *"People were enjoying banquets and parties and weddings right up to the time Noah entered his boat. People didn't realize what was going to happen until the flood came and swept them all away."* It appears that people were living their lives as they wanted without giving God or their actions a second thought. I don't think we are that far removed from those two items in our society today – evil thoughts and Godless living.

So, take heed. There is a lot more to the story of Noah than a big boat full of animals. It is a call for us to wake up and seek the Lord in our lives. A day will come when life on this earth, as we know it, will come to an end.

<u>We are in the Same Boat but God's Promises are Still True</u>

The other well-known part of Noah's story is the rainbow. What is the rainbow? It was given as a sign from God to remember His promise that He would never again destroy the earth with a flood. He has kept that promise. It was a promise of deliverance.

The other reference to the story of Noah's Ark in the New Testament is also a promise and a story of deliverance. *"Christ suffered for our sins once for all time. He never sinned, but he died for sinners to bring you safely home to God. He suffered physical death, but he was raised to life in the Spirit. So he went and preached to the spirits in prison—those who disobeyed God long ago when God waited patiently while Noah was building his boat. Only eight people were saved from drowning in that terrible flood. And that water is a picture of baptism, which now saves you, not by removing dirt from your body, but as a response to God from a clean conscience. It is effective because of the resurrection of Jesus Christ" (1 Peter 3:18-21, NLT).*

This passage has several interesting points, but let me break them down by the promises they contain. Just as God made a promise to Noah, He has also made some promises to us today.

- 1st Promise - He promises a dwelling place: *"But he died for sinners to bring you safely home to God" (1 Peter 3:18, NLT).* Do you remember God's reaction back in Genesis 6 when He saw what man had become? *"It broke His Heart."* God has a solution to the sinfulness of man – *"He died for sinners to bring you safely home to God"*

- 2nd Promise – He waits patiently: *"So he went and preached to the spirits in prison - those who disobeyed God long ago when God waited patiently while Noah was building his boat. Only eight people were saved from drowning in that terrible flood" (1 Peter 3:19,20, NLT).*

There are many ideas about this passage—here is my understanding: Jesus' spirit preached to the spirits of those who died in the flood and who had rejected God. This is consistent with God's broken heart. God waited 120 years in Noah's time to see if man would recognize Him. The only people that did were Noah and his family.

God is still waiting patiently today. *"But do not forget this one thing, dear friends: With the Lord, a day is like a thousand years, and a thousand years are like a day. The Lord is not slow in keeping his promise, as some understand slowness. He is patient with you, not wanting anyone to perish, but everyone to come to repentance" (2 Peter 3:8-9).* The actions of men still break the heart of God today. He is patiently waiting for men to come to Him.

Just as God has not broken His promise with the rainbow, neither will He break His promise of a dwelling place with Him. How do you claim that promise? Peter connects claiming that promise with baptism.

### How Do You Claim the Promises of God?

Baptism is one way to claim God's promises. It is a participation in the blessings of the resurrection: *"And that water is a picture of baptism, which now saves you, not by removing dirt from your body, but as a response to God from a clean conscience. It is effective because of the resurrection of Jesus Christ" (1 Peter 3:21).*

Baptism is a gift from God that allows someone to commit themselves to Jesus and all He has done for them. It is the beginning point of living a Christian life. It is a participation in the death, burial, and resurrection of Jesus. Baptism is about a clean conscience before God that can only come through the forgiveness of God. It is the resurrection of Jesus that gives it power.

I don't know about you, but the things I shared above never seemed to make it into the story of Noah's Ark when I was a kid. It is interesting and refreshing to see how the well-known story is more than "just a story." It is a picture of how we can find our way to dwell with God for eternity.

### Study Guide: Noah and Us - We are in the Same Boat!

Pray for God's guidance and insight as you study His Word. He knows your heart and what you need to learn.

### Focus Your Mind and Heart

What comes to mind when you think about Noah's Ark?

You don't have to be a fisherman or boater to understand the terminology in this chapter. What does it mean when someone says, "We're in this boat together?"

How much has the heart of man changed since the days of Noah?

### Examine the Word

Read Genesis 6 – 9 to get the whole story.

In Matthew 24:37-39 Jesus refers to the story of Noah in the context of His second coming. How are the story of Noah and His second coming related?

What "broke the heart of God" in Genesis 6:5-6? What do you think breaks the heart of God today?

God sent a rainbow as a sign of His promise not to destroy the earth again with a flood. The promises of God are good and special. What promises of God can be found in 1 Peter 3:18-21?

### Take a Look at Your Life

How should you respond to people who seem to have no regard for the things of God?

What are some of the promises God has blessed you with in life?

What is the foundation of these promises in your life?

**Apply it to Your Life**

Can you think of anyone you know personally who needs God in their life? If the answer is "yes," do the following:

1.    Pray for them daily that they will open their heart to God.
2.    Think of some practical ways that you can share the love of God with them.
3.    Invite them to attend a worship service, a small group meeting, or a one-on-one Bible study with you.

# CHAPTER SIX

## *Abraham's Call and Ours*

### Genesis 12:1-7

From my sophomore year in high school until my senior year, I wrestled with a question. What do I want to do with my life? It was a struggle because – well, what I decided would impact me for years to come. I had always been interested in architecture and took two years of vocational architectural classes in high school. I also knew that my dad wanted me to be an architect or design engineer. My dad was pretty quiet and didn't ever say much, but I knew that's what he wanted me to do. It was a struggle for me because, in my freshman and sophomore years, I became involved in our church youth group and was challenged to think about going to Bible College.

There were a lot of twists and turns in my thought process. One week, I would want to pursue the architectural route, and the next week, I would decide Bible College was the way to go. God never came to me in a booming voice with bright lights and angels saying, " JEFF— ENTER THE MINISTRY!" Quite frankly, it would have been easier if He had done that.

I've discovered that God rarely works that way – even in the Bible, He rarely worked that way. But there are defining moments – sometimes when you least expect them – that seem to confirm or direct us when we are really seeking him. For me, there were two defining moments. One was at a church camp during the evening worship time. The invitation was given at the end of the service, and I went forward and committed to going to Bible college for at least one year. There were times after that that I thought, "What was I thinking?" but it still remained one of those defining moments. The second was a conversation I had with my youth minister. He asked me a question that I could never get out of my mind – "Where do you think you will have the most impact for the kingdom, being an architect or being a minister?" That question rattled around in my head for a long time. Along the way other things happened but I responded to the call God put on my heart, left the "Holy Land" (Southern Indiana), and journeyed to a strange land called Illinois to attend Lincoln Christian College.

What is your story? What is your journey? It seems that God can tap us on the shoulder at any time in our lives and want us to do something. It doesn't happen just when we are in high school or college. He may have something for you to do now that you are retired that will impact the Kingdom. He may have something for you to do now that your kids are finally grown and out of the house. He may have something for you to do now that you are turning 40 and wondering how you got that old so fast. He may have something for you to do if you are in college pursuing a career and plotting out your future. If that moment happens, how will you respond to His call?

God has been tapping people on the shoulder for a long time. I want us to look at one of those taps that happened to a guy named Abram. His name was changed later to Abraham—you may know him more by that name. That is the name I will use in telling his story.

The story of the Patriarchs—Abraham, Isaac, and Jacob—took place in what is known as the "fertile crescent" approximately 2000 – 1700 BC. The fertile crescent is a portion of land that extends in an arch from Northern Israel to Iraq. The area is still heavily populated today.

Abraham was living at the north end of the fertile crescent in a town named Haran. The area today is still populated and located in South Central Turkey. Abraham's father and family came from the south and stopped in this area. It became Abraham's "hometown". When he wanted a wife for his son Isaac, he sent his servant back to Haran. When Abraham's grandchildren, Jacob and Esau, got into a fight, Jacob fled and went back to Haran. There he also found a wife, actually, two of them – but that's another story.

Haran was a nice place. It was a nice, fertile, green valley. Abraham's father had moved the family there from the area we now know as Iraq. Abraham grew up, married a woman named Sarai, and probably expected to live out his days there. That all changed one day when Abraham heard the call of God on his life. He wasn't a young man, even in those days. By the age of 75 years old, he had settled in, amassed a significant amount of wealth, and was probably well-known in the area. Then he had his "moment" with God: *"The Lord had said to Abram, 'Leave your native country, your relatives, and your father's family, and go to the land that I will show you. I will make you into a great nation. I will bless you and make you famous, and you will be a blessing to others. I will bless those who bless you and curse those who treat you with contempt. All the families on earth will be blessed through you'"* (Genesis 12:1 – 3).

This passage is known as the Abrahamic Covenant. What is a covenant? It is a promise between two parties. God made several covenants with man throughout the Bible. He always kept His side of the deal – that kind of covenant was called a unilateral covenant – meaning it would last forever.

This passage is one of the most significant covenants in the Bible. Why? It outlines God's redemptive story. As a professor I once had in college would say, "Other than that, it's insignificant!"

So, God comes to Abraham and says, "Hey Abraham, I've got a deal for you. Leave this place and go to a land that I will show you." What God says to Abraham and promises him becomes a major theme of the Bible. There are three major parts of the covenant, and those three parts outline the rest of the story in the Bible.

- Part 1 – Promise of a land – vs. 1 - *"go to the land that I will show you."*– Genesis through Judges deals with all the events leading up to and getting the Promise Land.
- Part 2 – Promise of a nation – vs. 2 – *"I will make you into a great nation."* – Ruth through Malachi is the story of the development of that nation, with its peak of power coming with David as King in 2 Samuel.
- Part 3 – Promise of a blessing to all the earth through his descendants – vs. 3 – *"All the families on earth will be blessed through you."* – This is the New Testament and the story of Jesus

God confirmed His covenant two other times in Genesis with Abraham - Genesis 15 & 17 and twice in Exodus, chapters 2 & 6. It is also confirmed again in Acts 3:25,26 when God is establishing the church. The fulfillment of those three promises throughout history formed the foundation for Christianity today. The "land", the "nation", and "the blessing" are still very much a part of what is happening in the world today. So much of what happens in the world, especially the Middle East, involves Israel. God's hand is still at work in history. The "blessing" that came through Christ shapes our faith and hope for eternal life. The Abrahamic Covenant may be "old news" but it certainly cannot be denied that it will shape a "new" future.

Could it be that God still calls people to leave some things behind and claim the promises He gives? He called Abraham to leave his home, his land, and the life he had established. How did He respond? *"So Abram departed as the Lord had instructed" (Genesis 12:4).*

## God Calls Us to Leave Things Behind

I don't know if you have ever felt God's call on your heart to pull up stakes and "go to a land that He will show you"? I can somewhat relate to this story when our family left central Illinois to move to Florida. Without going into all the details, I felt God put it on my heart to pursue a different ministry after spending twenty-eight wonderful years at a church in Springfield, Illinois. We moved to Bonita Springs, Florida and began a ministry at a smaller church with a different demographic. We left behind a beautiful home, a great church, wonderful friends and the security that goes along with all of that. It was an exciting time and scary time. It meant finding a place to live, making new friends and leading a new church that was very different from the one in Springfield. Both ministries have been a blessing in our lives, and we would never have gotten to enjoy God's blessings if we closed our ears to His calling.

God may not be calling you to move to a different city or state, but if we listen closely enough and pay attention to what is going on around us, God is always calling us to experience something new with Him. In order to experience His blessings, you might need to leave some things behind. He might be opening a door that leads to a new job. He might open a door for a new start in a different town or different state. He might put someone in your path who needs your help. Don't tune out what God may be saying to you. Those things might possibly mean a sacrifice on your part, but rest assured, God will be faithful on His part.

## With God's Call, Comes God's Promises

When God called Abraham to leave his country and people to go to a new land, He did it with promises attached. You can see God's hand on Abraham throughout the story of Genesis. He was with Abraham and all his descendants. Did Abraham and his descendants always do everything right? No. Did God totally abandon them when they needed Him the most? No. God was faithful to the promises He made to Abraham and brought them to fulfillment.

It is encouraging to reflect on the promises God gives us in His Word. Do we deserve them because we always do everything right? No. Does He give up on us? No. Read through a small sampling of the promises of God and be reminded of how He can take the "old" and make it "new" again:

- In Matthew 11:28 Jesus says: *"Come to me, all you who are weary and burdened, and I will give you rest."* He calls us to leave our labor and our burdens and come to the rest He offers.
- The apostle Peter declares in 1 Peter 2:9: *"You are a chosen people, a royal priesthood, a holy nation, a people belonging to God, that you may declare the praises of him who called you out of darkness into his wonderful light."* He calls us to leave the darkness of this world and come to live in the light as a chosen people.
- John says in John 14:1-3: *"Do not let your hearts be troubled. Trust in God; trust also in me. In my Father's house are many rooms; if it were not so, I would have told you. I am going there to prepare a place for you."*
- The Apostle Paul shares a promise in 2 Corinthians 5:17: *"Therefore, if anyone is in Christ, he is a new creation; the old has gone, the new has come!"*

Is God calling you to leave some things so that you can enjoy the promises He has given? Several years ago, a woman was sitting in the congregation I was preaching to, and she had a defining moment. She felt God tap her on the shoulder and call her to leave everything she knew and answer His call. She left her comfortable job and home and became a missionary in Haiti. God blessed that calling and she became the overseer of several feeding and educational programs that impacted a lot of Haitian families. Her openness and willingness to hear God and trust in His promises is a great example of a modern-day Abraham.

What does God have for you to do? I encourage you to always be open to His touch in your life. You never know when it might just make a difference for eternity!

## Study Guide: Abraham's Call and Ours

Pray for God's guidance and insight as you study His Word. He knows your heart and what you need to learn.

### Focus Your Mind and Heart

What are some of the big decisions that you have had to make in life?

Did any of those decisions change the direction of your life? If so, how?

What are some of the promises that you have counted on to get you through life?

### Examine the Word

What are the three things that God promised Abraham in Genesis 12:1-3?

How do those three promises help shape the story of the Bible?

God not only gave promises to Abraham, but He also gave promises to us. Examine the following passages and write out the promises He makes to you:

- Matthew 11:28
- 1 Peter 2:9

What are some other promises He gives us?

### Take a Look at Your Life

Have you ever had a "defining moment" in life? If so, what was it?

God sometimes prompts us to do something special in life. It may be something big, or it may be something small. How should you respond when you feel that prompting of God in your life?

### Apply it to Your Life

The most important thing in this chapter is to see how God wants to be a part of the story of your life. What is your story? If you are a follower of Jesus, write out your story. This story can become your testimony to share with someone else. Take your story and try condensing it to a 30-second story that you can quickly share with others. Use it as an opening for sharing your faith.

# CHAPTER SEVEN

## *Sodom & Gomorrah - Don't Be Fooled*

**Genesis 13-19; 2 Peter 2, 3; Luke 17:24-29**

In this chapter you will find one of those stories that you have heard about but may not have examined in too much detail. Let's look at the story. It starts in Genesis 13 with Abraham and Lot.

We find that Abraham had taken his nephew Lot with him into the land which God directed him to. Like Abraham, Lot owned his own livestock and had several herdsmen and their families that traveled with him. Both clans grew so large that the land where they were staying became too small to sustain both groups. Things finally came to a head when quarreling broke out between Abraham's herdsmen and Lot's herdsmen. Abraham and Lot had a meeting, and Abraham proposed that they go their separate ways. Abraham was very gracious and gave Lot the first choice of land in which he wanted to live. It was at that point that Lot had a decision to make. He seemed to take the best of what was offered, at least on the surface:

*Genesis 13:10,11 - "Lot looked up and saw that the whole plain of the Jordan was well watered, like the garden of the Lord, like the land of Egypt, toward Zoar. (This was before the Lord destroyed Sodom and Gomorrah.) So Lot chose for himself the whole plain of the Jordan and set out toward the east."*

He may not have made the best choice. Why? Listen to verse 13: *"Now the men of Sodom were wicked and were sinning greatly against the Lord." (Genesis 13:13).*

We are not sure how much time passed and how long Lot lived in Sodom and Gomorrah, but after a period of time, Abraham re-enters the story. God sent some men, who were angels, to remind Abraham of the covenant God made in Genesis 12: a land, a nation, and a blessing. After they affirmed the covenant, they began to continue their journey to deliver the judgment of God on Sodom and

Gomorrah. This is what happened: Genesis 18:20-24 - *"Then the Lord said, 'The outcry against Sodom and Gomorrah is so great and their sin so grievous that I will go down and see if what they have done is as bad as the outcry that has reached me. If not, I will know.'"*

When Abraham heard this, knowing that is where his nephew Lot lived, he started plea bargaining with God. *"Will you sweep away the righteous with the wicked? What if there are fifty righteous people in the city?" (Genesis 18:23,24).* Abraham must have known what kind of place it was because he was not comfortable with the number fifty. He pleads with God to spare the people there, counting all the way down to ten people before he stops. The angel told him that the place would not be destroyed for the sake of ten people. Come to find out, God could not find ten righteous people.

How wicked of a place was it? The two men (angels) go to Sodom, and Lot happens to greet them at the city gate. In that culture, the elders of the city and the leaders of the community sat at the gate during the day. The question that pops into my mind is, "Had Lot become one of the leading men in the city?" Another question, "Once Lot saw what kind of place he had chosen, why did he stay?" We don't really know the answers to those questions, but they might be important for us to consider in our own lives. Do we sometimes dwell in places that are not the best for us?

Lot invites them to stay at his home. As their evening together was coming to a close, a disturbance occurred outside: *"Before they had gone to bed, all the men from every part of the city of Sodom — both young and old — surrounded the house. They called to Lot, "Where are the men who came to you tonight? Bring them out to us so that we can have sex with them." (Genesis 19:4-5).* Lot refused to do what they had requested and tried to reason with them. They were beyond the point of reasoning and started to attack him. The two men (angels) opened the door, pulled him to safety, and then struck all the men outside the door with blindness.

Then the two men (angels) said this to Lot: *"Do you have anyone else here - sons-in-law, sons, or daughters, or anyone else in the city who belongs to you? Get them out of here, because we are going to destroy this place. The outcry to the Lord against its people is so great that he has sent us to destroy it" (Genesis 19:12-13).* Then this is what happened: *"By the time Lot reached Zoar, the sun had risen over the land. Then the Lord rained down burning sulfur on Sodom and Gomorrah — from the Lord out of the heavens" (Genesis 19:23-26).*

Let's go back to Lot's original decision and see how it applies to us. Lot had a choice about which way he would go. His choice made a big difference in his life. Look again at Lot's decision: *"Lot looked up and saw that the whole plain of the Jordan was well watered, like the garden of the Lord. So Lot chose for himself the whole plain of the Jordan and set out toward the east"* (Genesis 13:10, 11). There are some good lessons to be learned from the story of Lot.

### Don't be Fooled by a Mirage

Do you know what a mirage is? You see something that looks great, but it turns out it is not what you thought it was. A couple of years ago, Judy and I took a trip to Alaska. We planned the trip on our own and made all our reservations for housing. We selected some Airbnb's and were a little skeptical of how nice they would be. In Valdez, AK, we broke away from the AirBnB route and booked a hotel room. We thought, "If all the other places are not nice, at least we will have a night in a good hotel." What we saw online and what the hotel was really like were worlds apart. The room had a small 12" TV, the heating and cooling duct was one continuous line between the rooms with no individual control, and the bathroom was almost big enough to turn around in! The website was very misleading, a "mirage" of what the room really was.

Have you ever been fooled by a mirage in life? Life offers all kinds of images that look good, but in reality, they are not good. Lot looked at the valley of Sodom and Gomorrah and thought it looked good. It wasn't. It was a place full of sin and pain. A lesson to be learned is: Don't be fooled by a mirage in life that the devil puts in front of you. Check out what you see with the Word of God – it may save you a lot of grief.

### Don't Be Fooled by the World: Listen to God

We find the Apostle Peter referring to this story in his second letter. Peter warns the Christians against those who bring false teachings to the church and uses the story of Sodom and Gomorrah as an example. False teachers were painting a false picture and teaching the early Christians that they could do whatever they wanted in their lifestyle, do whatever they wanted with their bodies, etc. The world was telling them that none of it mattered; everything would be fine.

Peter addresses that and gives a teaching about the judgment of God and the hope God offers: *"If He (God) did not spare the ancient world when he brought the flood on its ungodly people, but protected Noah, a preacher of righteousness, and seven others; if he condemned the cities of Sodom and Gomorrah by burning them to ashes, and made them an example of what is going to happen to the ungodly; and if he rescued Lot, a righteous man, who was distressed by the filthy lives of lawless men (for that righteous man, living among them day after day, was tormented in his righteous soul by the lawless deeds he saw and heard)— if this is so, then the Lord knows how to rescue godly men from trials and to hold the unrighteous for the day of judgment, while continuing their punishment"* (2 Peter 2:5-10).

He is encouraging the Christians and getting them to see two things: 1) God will bring judgment to evil men and people who follow their ways. What they were doing in Sodom and Gomorrah was wrong; it was a sin, and it can't be rationalized away. 2) God will rescue those who remain faithful to Him, even if they live in the midst of evil. He gives us a message of hope. That is why Peter uses the story of Noah and the story of Lot. God saved both of them from the evil around them.

Once again, the New Testament uses an Old Testament story to bring a message of hope and redemption. Peter delivers a message of God's grace in the midst of judgment. Listen to what he says about this in chapter three of his letter: *"But do not forget this one thing, dear friends: With the Lord a day is like a thousand years, and a thousand years are like a day. The Lord is not slow in keeping his promise, as some understand slowness. He is patient with you, not wanting anyone to perish, but everyone to come to repentance. But the day of the Lord will come like a thief. The heavens will disappear with a roar, the elements will be destroyed by fire, and the earth and everything in it will be laid bare"* (2 Peter 3:8-10).

If Peter's letter had stopped there, we would be in a mess. When you read those verses, hopefully, one thing pops into your head: "Help! What do I do?" Peter goes on to answer that question: *"Since everything will be destroyed in this way, what kind of people ought you to be? You ought to live holy and godly lives as you look forward to the day of God and speed its coming. That day will bring about the destruction of the heavens by fire, and the elements will melt in the heat. But in keeping with his promise we are looking forward to a new heaven and a new earth, the home of righteousness. So then, dear friends, since you are looking forward to this, make every effort to be found spotless, blameless and at peace with him. Bear in mind that our Lord's patience means salvation" (2 Peter 3:11-15).*

There are plenty of false teachings in our world today. There are a lot of false teachings about human sexuality and the way God created males and females. You will find numerous false teachings that tell us we can rationalize any type of behavior in the name of love. Many teach that you can find fulfillment in life through the pursuit of wealth or sexual gratification.

Just as it was in the days of Noah, just as it was with Sodom and Gomorrah, so it is and will be with us in the eyes of God. The Bible is honest with us, and I appreciate that. We must not write it off as "old fashioned" or "irrelevant." Just as God is the same "yesterday, today, and forever," so is His Word.

The second major reference to the Old Testament story of Sodom & Gomorrah in the New Testament is from the lips of Jesus.

<u>Don't be Fooled by Living Just for the Moment – Jesus is Coming Again</u>

What do we know about the future? We can't know everything, but we can know some things. We know that we can count on what Jesus has to say – especially when He speaks of His return:

*"For the Son of Man in his day will be like the lightning, which flashes and lights up the sky from one end to the other. But first he must suffer many things and be rejected by this generation. Just as it was in the days of Noah, so also will it be in the days of the Son of Man" (Luke 17:24-25).*

*"It was the same in the days of Lot. People were eating and drinking, buying and selling, planting and building. But the day Lot left Sodom, fire and sulfur rained down from heaven and destroyed them all" (Luke 17:28-29).*

I once heard a minister say there are two different ways to preach about people dying and going to hell. Those ways apply to this teaching. One way is to preach it like you are excited about it: "Wow, this is great! Bring down the hail, fire, and brimstone, and watch all those sinners burn!" The other way is to share it with tears in your eyes and a broken heart because people have turned their backs on God's grace and forgiveness.

My preference is the latter. Let's go back to that verse we read earlier: "*The Lord is not slow in keeping his promise, as some understand slowness. He is patient with you, not wanting anyone to perish, but everyone to come to repentance*" *(2 Peter 3:9)*. The story of Sodom and Gomorrah is one that breaks the heart of God. It should also break our hearts today. It is not just the story of Sodom and Gomorrah but also the story that so many people around us are writing today.

God wants us to stand up for what is right and live lives that honor Him. In doing so, though, we cannot close our eyes to those who are living lives that are not pleasing to God and have our hearts broken. That brokenness should compel us to share the love of Jesus with those who do not know Him.

## Study Guide: Sodom & Gomorrah - Don't Be Fooled

Pray for God's guidance and insight as you study His Word. He knows your heart and what you need to learn.

### Focus Your Mind and Heart

What is a mirage?

Maybe you have heard that saying, "Fool me once, shame on you. Fool me twice, shame on me." How does it make you feel if someone "fools you"?

Where do people turn if they need information about something in today's world?

How can you be sure that the information you are getting from various sources is correct?

### Examine the Word

Read Genesis 18-19 again. What kind of place do you picture Sodom and Gomorrah to be?

How does 2 Peter 2:5-10 bring a message of hope and redemption?

Peter talks about the patience of God in 2 Peter 3:8-10. Why is God being patient with mankind?

One day His patience will run out. What will happen then?

Even though the world we live in reflects some of the things found in Sodom and Gomorrah, what is God's desire for us today?

What do we have to look forward to from 2 Peter 3:11-15?

### Take a Look at Your Life

This chapter says not to be fooled by a mirage or the world or just living for the moment. Which one of those things is your weak spot?

What do you look forward to about the return of Jesus?

What is your "gut reaction" when you hear that people are dying and going to hell?

### Apply it to Your Life

List 3 ways that you can strengthen your faith to help you not be fooled by Satan.

Write a letter to someone you know who needs Jesus. Share His message of love and salvation for them.

# CHAPTER EIGHT

## *Moses and the Burning Bush and the Power of "I AM"*

**Exodus 3:1-15, John 8:24, 28, 58; 9:5; 10:7-11; 14:6**

As we continue looking at Old Testament stories and seeing their significance in the New Testament, we are moving out of the book of Genesis and venturing into the book of Exodus. The book of Exodus tells us the story of the Children of Israel. We find the story of Moses and the "roller coaster ride of a life" he had in Egypt and the journey in the wilderness. Exodus contains the miraculous story of the crossing of the Red Sea and the faithfulness and unfaithfulness of the Children of Israel.

The main character in Exodus is Moses, the third most mentioned person in the Bible, with 803 mentions. (Just in case you are curious: David is second with 974. Jesus is first with 1310 times.) In this chapter, we will look at a significant event in Moses's life that is used in a special way in the New Testament.

The story of Moses and the burning bush is found in Exodus 3. Let's read the story, and then we will look at some specific verses.

*"Now Moses was tending the flock of Jethro his father-in-law, the priest of Midian, and he led the flock to the far side of the desert and came to Horeb, the mountain of God. There the angel of the Lord appeared to him in flames of fire from within a bush. Moses saw that though the bush was on fire it did not burn up. So Moses thought, 'I will go over and see this strange sight — why the bush does not burn up.' When the Lord saw that he had gone over to look, God called to him from within the bush, 'Moses! Moses!' And Moses said, 'Here I am.' 'Do not come any closer,' God said. 'Take off your sandals, for the place where you are standing is holy ground.' Then he said, 'I am the God of your father, the God of Abraham, the God of Isaac and the God of Jacob.' At this, Moses hid his face, because he was afraid to look at God" (Exodus 3:1-4).*

God then tells Moses that He has heard the cry of His people from

Egypt and that He is going to rescue them. He says to Moses: *"'So now, go. I am sending you to Pharaoh to bring my people the Israelites out of Egypt.' But Moses said to God, 'Who am I, that I should go to Pharaoh and bring the Israelites out of Egypt?' And God said, 'I will be with you. And this will be the sign to you that it is I who have sent you: When you have brought the people out of Egypt, you will worship God on this mountain.' Moses said to God, 'Suppose I go to the Israelites and say to them, 'The God of your fathers has sent me to you,' and they ask me, 'What is his name?' Then what shall I tell them?'"* (Exodus 3:10-13).

Is Moses just looking for excuses, or does He really not understand who is sending Him? Maybe a little of both. But basically, Moses knew the Israelites would want to know by what authority Moses did his work. So, here is how God answers Moses' question: "Who should I tell them sent me?": *"God said to Moses, 'I AM WHO I AM. This is what you are to say to the Israelites: 'I AM has sent me to you.'"* (Exodus 3:14).

The answer God gives is significant. It is a new designation for God. God's name, "Jehovah," had been known for centuries and was familiar to the patriarchs (14:22; 15:1; 25:21-22; 28:13; 49:18). What Moses asked was, "What does Your name mean? What kind of a God are You?" God's answer becomes a lasting designation of His eternal power.

Jehovah, one of the well-known names of God, is a dynamic one based on the Hebrew verb "to be" or "to become." He is the self-existent one who always was, always is, and always will be the faithful and dependable God who calls Himself "I AM." He goes on to clarify it for Moses: God also said to Moses, *"Say to the Israelites, 'The Lord, the God of your fathers — the God of Abraham, the God of Isaac and the God of Jacob — has sent me to you.' This is my name forever, the name by which I am to be remembered from generation to generation"* (Exodus 3:15).

After this exchange, the chapter continues with God giving him some detailed instructions. In Chapter Four, we see God having to convince Moses to do what God told him to do. I encourage you to read the rest of Exodus 3 and 4 to get these details.

"I am that I am" is a declaration of divine power and control of all things. The phrase becomes significant in the New Testament when Jesus uses it in reference to Himself. Let's see how Jesus takes this Old Testament phrase and makes it new again. I could get technical about all of this and go into the verb forms and the Hebrew and Greek languages, but if we do all that, I think we would miss the point. I want us to simply see Jesus as God: the same yesterday, today, and forever. A God that is not limited by time or power but eternal and all-powerful.

## See the Power of the "I AM" in Dominance Over Creation

The first New Testament usage of the Old Testament phrase is found in John 6:19-20. It comes with Jesus' walking to the disciples on the water. He uses the Greek word for the Hebrew designation of God found in Exodus 3:14. *"They saw Jesus walking on the sea... and they were frightened. But he said to them, 'It is 'I AM'; do not be afraid.'"* (*John 6:19-20*).

It is the great "I AM" who comes walking to the disciples on the sea. Jesus demonstrated that He is over, greater than, and more powerful than all of creation by walking on the water and saying to the disciples in the boat, "You want to know who I am? I Am Who I Am. I can walk on this stuff I created."

Reflect for a moment on the power of Jesus – the Great "I AM." He is more powerful than creation. The one who has the power over creation is the same one who says, *"Come to me, all you who are weary and burdened, and I will give you rest"* (*Matthew 11:28*).

## See the Power of the "I AM" in His Authority

He is more powerful than any authority on Earth. When Judas and the Roman soldiers came to arrest Jesus in the Garden of Gethsemane, He said to them, - *"'Whom do you seek?' They answered 'Jesus of Nazareth.' Jesus answered, 'I am He.' ... when Jesus said to them 'I am He,' they retreated and fell to the ground... Jesus answered 'I told you that I am He'"* (*John 18:6-8*).

Jesus demonstrated His power over the authorities of His day. Pilate may have had the power to sentence Jesus to death, but he didn't have the power to keep Him in the grave. Jesus is more powerful than any authority on earth. We need to learn to submit to the power of the great "I AM."

## Apply His Power in Your Daily Life with the "I am" Statements of Jesus

Hear Him say to you, "I am the bread of Life." Bread has been a staple of mankind's life for thousands of generations. Jesus says that He is *"the bread of life" (John 6:35)*. Just as bread sustains our physical needs, Jesus satisfies our spiritual hunger and thirst. Generation after generation has sought to fill a "God-sized hole" in their lives. Jesus is the only solution that can fill the void man has.

Hear Him say to you, "I am the light of the World." Jesus is the light of the world (John 8:12). Darkness can never overpower light. The only way for darkness to exist is for the light to be removed. Do you feel you are in a dark place in your life? If you are, the reason is that you have removed the light where it is needed most.

Hear Him say to you, "I am the gate." Jesus is the gate (John 10:9). If you want to find protection from your enemies –whoever or whatever they may be, Jesus offers a place of refuge and protection. Jesus goes on to say: *"They will come in and go out, and find pasture. The thief comes only to steal and kill and destroy; I have come that they may have life, and have it to the full" (John 10:9b,10)*. There is a lot of advice out there that tells you how to keep your "stuff" secure. Jesus made the offer long ago for your life – "Let me be the gatekeeper of your soul. Let me give you the life that will last forever."

Hear Him say to you, "I am the good shepherd." Jesus is the good shepherd (John 10:11, 14). I don't need to elaborate much on what a shepherd does for His sheep—He does everything for them. Likewise, Jesus cares for us as His sheep. Jesus says in John 10:14, *"I know my sheep, and my sheep know me."*

Hear Him say to you, *"I am the resurrection and the life" (John 11:25)*. He conquers death and gives you eternal life. When Martha confronted Jesus and blamed Him for the death of her brother Lazarus, she said, *"If you had been here, he wouldn't have died."* Then Jesus calmly said, *"I am the resurrection and the life. The one who believes in me will live, even though they die."* Is that powerful or what?

Hear Him say to you, "I am the way, the truth, the life." Jesus is the way, the truth, and the life (John 14:6). The world would have you believe that there are many ways to get to heaven. Jesus said there is one way, and the road that goes to heaven is through Him. Do you know what road you are on?

Hear Him say to you, "I am the vine." Jesus is the true vine (John 15:1). The first house we owned in Illinois had a fence around the backyard. On the east side of the yard, the fence had this ugly vine growing through it. I cut the vine where it came through the fence. A couple of weeks later, my new neighbor, whom I had not met up to that point, came out to talk to me, and he wasn't very happy. Why? I had cut the grapevine that he had nurtured along the top of the fence. Everything died beyond the point where I had cut it. Why? Because its source of life had been cut off.

Do you want to know how to thrive in life? Jesus said in John 15: *"I am the vine; you are the branches. If you remain in me and I in you, you will bear much fruit; apart from me you can do nothing."* He sustains us and produces fruit in us.

Let the "I AM" Make a Difference in Your Life

When I was younger, I heard a woman at a Billy Graham crusade say something I have never forgotten: "There is nothing too great for the power of God and nothing too small for His love." That is a good image of the great "I AM."

The Old and New Testaments show us a God who is powerful enough to speak through a burning bush and personal enough to know the needs of His children. When Jesus said in John 14:6, *"I am the way and the truth and the life. No one comes to the Father except through Me,"* He wanted us to let Him make a difference in our lives. In a world with many voices crying out for your attention, don't miss the voice that makes a difference for eternity.

## Study Guide: Moses and the Burning Bush
## and the Power of the "I AM"

Pray for God's guidance and insight as you study His Word. He knows your heart and what you need to learn.

### Focus Your Mind and Heart

Describe a time when you were asked to do something but weren't sure if you could do it or not.

Who is the most powerful person in the world? Where does the power come from?

Who is someone who has made a big difference in your life?

### Examine the Word

Chapter 8 uses many scripture passages, but they all point to the same thing—The Great "I AM." What is so significant about that designation of God?

What do you think are some of the emotions that Moses had when He encountered God in the burning bush? (Exodus 3:1-4)

In Exodus 3:10-15 what stands out to you about the heart of God? What stands out to you about the heart of Moses? What does God do for reluctant servants?

In John 6:19-20 Jesus is the "I AM" when He walks on water. Why is it important to Jesus as one having power over creation?

In the Garden of Gethsemane, Jesus declared, "I AM He," and the ones who came to arrest Him fell to the ground (John 18:6-8). Why do you think they did that?

The following passages are known as the "Seven I AM" statements of Jesus. Just read them and let God impress upon your heart who He is.

- I am the Bread of Life – John 6:35

- I am the Light of the World – John 8:12
- I am the Gate – John 10:9
- I am the Good Shepherd – John 10:11,14
- I am the Resurrection and the Life – John 11:25
- I am the Way, the Truth, and the Life – John 14:6
- I am the Vine – John 15:1

**Take a Look at Your Life**

How many times have you felt prompted by God to do something for Him, but you were hesitant to do so?

What difference should it make in your life when you see that the "I AM" of the Old Testament is also the "I AM" of the New Testament?

How can that make a difference in your life today?

**Apply it to Your Life**

Take the seven "I AM" statements listed above and write one or two sentences about what each one means to you personally.

Make it a goal to memorize the seven "I AM" statements.

# CHAPTER NINE

## *The Power of Passover*

**Exodus 11 & 12; Matthew 26**

Do you have any family traditions regarding special meals during the year, like at Christmas or Thanksgiving? When I was a young boy, our family would always go to our grandparents' house to have that turkey dinner. At Christmas, we would always read the Christmas story together before opening gifts. You might remember a special dish or tradition you had in your family.

Those types of traditions have been around for a very long time. As we continue with "The Old Made New," we are going to look at an Old Testament meal that took on special meaning in the New Testament. You've probably heard of the meals before—Passover and the Last Supper. Many Jews and Christians around the world still participate in these special meals.

### A Bit of Background

When the Passover meal was instituted, the Children of Israel were at the end of a 400-year stay in Egypt. For most of those years, they were slaves to the Pharaohs of Egypt. How did the Israelites become slaves in Egypt? At the end of the book of Genesis, we see that they moved to Egypt as a family of 70 because of a famine in the land. Joseph, a son of Jacob, had risen to second in command in Egypt but the providence of God. The people were saved from the famine, but when a new Pharaoh arose, he enslaved the Children of Israel. They were slaves for 400 years and God heard their cry for deliverance.

God then raises Moses to lead the people out of Egypt and confront Pharaoh. In Exodus, we find the story of the 10 plagues that God brought on the land of Egypt—Exodus 7 – 13. By the end of the 10th plague, Pharaoh and the Egyptians were happy to get rid of them. It was the 10th plague that was the catalyst for the Passover meal.

The Power of the Passover in the OT

What brought about the Passover? Moses confronted Pharaoh and told him to let the people go. Pharaoh refused, and God sent plagues on the land. After nine plagues, Pharaoh still refused. The tenth plague finally convinced him. This is how it was described: *"Every firstborn son in Egypt will die, from the firstborn son of Pharaoh, who sits on the throne, to the firstborn son of the female slave, who is at her hand mill, and all the firstborn of the cattle as well" (Exodus 11:5)*. When those words came to pass, here is what happened: *"During the night Pharaoh summoned Moses and Aaron and said, 'Up! Leave my people, you and the Israelites! Go, worship the Lord as you have requested'" (Exodus 12:31)*. That night of death and despair for the Egyptians is where we get what is called the Passover meal.

Why is it called Passover? It was a meal, but it is called the "Passover" because of what happened on that night. God gave the Children of Israel specific instructions for the meal. The elements of that meal came to have very special meanings. They were to take a lamb without blemish, kill the lamb, and prepare it for a special meal. They were to take the blood of the lamb that was slain and put it on the sides and tops of the doorframes. Then, the family would gather to eat the meal of the lamb that night.

What would the blood do? Exodus 12:13 explains: *"The blood will be a sign for you on the houses where you are, and when I see the blood, I will pass over you. No destructive plague will touch you when I strike Egypt."* The meal they would participate in that night would become known as the Passover meal because the angel that brought death to all the Egyptian firstborns would "pass" "over" any house that was marked by the blood of the lamb.

Why do it every year? Here is what Exodus: *"This is a day you are to commemorate; for the generations to come you shall celebrate it as a festival to the Lord—a lasting ordinance . . . because it was on this very day that I brought your divisions out of Egypt . . . And when your children ask you, 'What does this ceremony mean to you?' then tell them, 'It is the Passover sacrifice to the Lord, who passed over the houses of the Israelites in Egypt and spared our homes when he struck down the Egyptians.' Then the people bowed down and worshiped" (Exodus 12:14, 17, 26-27)*.

Did you catch that last phrase? One thing we need to understand about Passover is that it was not just a meal; it was a worship service.

*"Then the people bowed down and worshiped."* The Passover meal has been a part of the Jewish faith and practice ever since.

That is a very quick overview of the Passover meal. There is much more to it, but that gives us a picture of its origin and some of the significant symbolism. At least a couple of thousands of years transpired between the first Passover and the life of Jesus.

Passover was still a powerful event in every Jewish family during Jesus's time. Jesus used that Passover meal to mark a major transition in God's plan for mankind. So, let's look at Passover in the New Testament and how it impacts us today.

<u>The Power of the Passover is Seen in the Last Supper</u>

We see Jesus participating in the Passover meal at the end of the Gospels. It is commonly referred to as "The Last Supper." What happened at that Passover meal began what we call "Communion" today. We observe communion every Sunday during our worship services at the church where I serve. It is based on what happened at the Passover meal Jesus led before His death, which has become known as the "Last Supper."

The Power of the Last Supper Passover – our communion - marks a new beginning for those who know Jesus, the Lamb of God. The Passover and the escape from Egypt were powerful and pivotal points in God's story in the Old Testament. Likewise, the Last Supper Passover was a pivotal point in God's story in the New Testament and ours as we partake of Communion today.

It all began as any other Passover meal for the disciples. *"On the first day of the Feast of Unleavened Bread, the disciples came to Jesus and asked, 'Where do you want us to make preparations for you to eat the Passover?'"* (Matthew 26:17). They were going to go about their business in preparation for Passover, just like they had done all their lives. But Jesus knew that it was not going to be just another Passover meal: *"He replied, 'Go into the city to a certain man and tell him, 'The Teacher says: My appointed time is near. I am going to celebrate the Passover with my disciples at your house'"* (Matthew 28:18).

There is a key phrase in that verse: *"My appointed time is near."* It was one of those phrases that went right over the disciples' heads. Later that night, when Jesus shared that Passover meal with His disciples, He put something brand new into motion. He made a "New

Covenant" with God's people.

The "New Covenant" was a new agreement. A new way of doing things. *"And he took bread, gave thanks and broke it, and gave it to them, saying, 'This is my body given for you; do this in remembrance of me.' In the same way, after the supper he took the cup, saying, 'This cup is the new covenant in my blood, which is poured out for you'"* (Luke 22:19-21). At this point, Jesus went off script and changed thousands of years of tradition.

The bread that was used to signify events in the OT Passover story now took on a new meaning. It was now representative of His body that would be broken. The cup no longer was to remind them of the lamb's blood on the doorpost but rather His blood on the cross. No longer would the sacrifice of animals be required for the forgiveness of sins.

Anyone who accepts Christ and the sacrifice of His body and blood has a new beginning in life. The apostle Paul says that a person is a new creation; the old has gone, and the new has come.

## The Power of the Last Supper Passover is that it Creates a New Future

Matthew records the last words Jesus said that evening at the end of the Passover meal: *"I tell you, I will not drink of this fruit of the vine from now on until that day when I drink it anew with you in my Father's kingdom"* (Matthew 26:29). Jesus really goes off script here. Jesus is taking that which had been practiced for thousands of years by Jewish families, and He is totally changing it. He adds something to the Passover - a promise. One day, we will celebrate this meal together in heaven.

You see, the Old Testament Passover meal didn't contain any promises; it only reflected on the past and let you celebrate it in the present. Jesus now adds something totally new to the thinking. There is a wonderful promise for the future. A future celebration in heaven. That celebration is going to be something: a beautiful reunion, a time of rejoicing.

Jesus uses all the traditional elements of the Passover meal to paint a picture of eternity. In just a few hours after they finished that final Passover, He would be the lamb sacrificed, and His blood would be the blood that brought forgiveness of sins.

Just as God did everything that was needed to lead His people out of the bondage of slavery in Egypt, He did everything necessary for us to be set free from the slavery of sin and make heaven open for us. His body was broken. His blood was shed. Those things now free us, and we can rejoice in them every time we partake in communion. Those things point us to eternal life.

### The Power of the Last Supper Passover Can be Experienced Today

The next time you take part in communion, take some time to reflect on the power of Passover and the Communion of today. Communion is a time to reflect on the work of God. The Passover meal was a time to remember the angel of death passing over the houses of the Children of Israel and the exodus out of Egypt – God's deliverance. Communion is a time to reflect on the forgiveness God offers through the blood that was shed on the cross – it is that sacrifice that delivers us from the slavery of sin.

Communion is a time to rest in the promises of God. He gives us the promise of forgiveness. He gives us the promise of eternal life.

Communion is a time to rejoice for the love of God. At the cross, we come face to face with the love God had for us. It is John 3:16 being acted out in real life: *"For God so loved the world that he gave his one and only Son, that whoever believes in him shall not perish but have eternal life."*

So, when partaking in Communion, celebrate it as an act of worship. We have been partaking in Communion because of the power of the Passover—the power of God's new covenant that Jesus proclaimed on that night of the "Last Supper."

## Study Guide: The Power of Passover

Pray for God's guidance and insight as you study His Word. He knows your heart and what you need to learn.

### Focus Your Mind and Heart

What are some of your favorite holiday meals and traditions?

What do you know about the Jewish Passover meal?

Different churches practice communion differently. What is the tradition that you are most familiar with?

### Examine the Word

Exodus 12:13 says: *"The blood will be a sign for you on the houses where you are, and when I see the blood, I will pass over you. No destructive plague will touch you when I strike Egypt."* What is the significance of the blood? Why did there have to be shedding of blood? See Hebrews 9:22.

How often was Passover to be celebrated? What does this say about the significance of the ceremony? (Exodus 12:14,17, 26-27).

How was the Passover more than just another meal for a Jewish family?

The Passover that Jesus shared with His disciples was a "new covenant" (Luke 22:19-21). What was "new" about it? What were some of the common elements that received new meaning at the Last Supper?

The Passover, for centuries, directed the people's attention to what God had done in the past. Jesus changed the script when He shared the Passover/Last Supper with His disciples. What did He shift the focus to (Matthew 26:29)?

### Take a Look at Your Life

Why do you think Jesus used the Passover as a template for what He shared at the Last Supper?

Today, we remember what happened the night of the Last Supper by partaking in communion. How does partaking of communion impact you?

Spend a few minutes pondering the future aspect of sharing communion with Jesus in heaven. What do you think it will be like?

The next time you take part in communion, what are some of the things you will focus on?

How can you celebrate the "power of God" in communion?

### Apply it to Your Life

Write down some of the promises of God that you can reflect on while sharing in communion.

How will communion become a more meaningful act of worship in your life?

In the church I serve in we have a "communion meditation" prior to taking communion. The purpose of the communion meditation is to help people focus on the meaning of communion. Try writing a "communion meditation" that helps you focus on the meaning of communion.

# CHAPTER TEN

## Overcoming Doubt

### Jonah 1-4; Matthew 12:38-41; John 20

There is an interesting Old Testament story that is very well known, but it is rarely thought of as a lesson in the New Testament. It is the story of Jonah. What is Jonah known for? Right, being swallowed by a whale – or "great fish," as the text says.

Just to refresh our memory, let's quickly review the story. God told Jonah to go and preach to the wicked town of Nineveh. He didn't want to do what God told him to do and headed out of town on a boat to get as far away as he could. While on the boat, a big storm came up, he was thrown overboard and had a three-day cruise in the belly of a whale. He was spit onto dry ground and then went and preached to the Ninevites.

How does Jesus use the story in the New Testament? Let me set the scene. Jesus heals a demon-possessed man who was blind and mute. This got the attention of the people, and they said, "Could this be the son of David?" Which meant, could this be the Messiah the Jews had been waiting for? When the Pharisees heard this, they didn't like it. They accused Jesus of using the power of Satan to perform miracles. Jesus comes right back at them and blows their accusation right out of the water. Some of them hang around and try to cast more doubt in the minds of the people listening.

Here is what happens as recorded in Matthew 12:38-41: *"Then some of the Pharisees and teachers of the law said to him, 'Teacher, we want to see a miraculous sign from you.' He answered, 'A wicked and adulterous generation asks for a miraculous sign! But none will be given it except the sign of the prophet Jonah. For as Jonah was three days and three nights in the belly of a huge fish, so the Son of Man will be three days and three nights in the heart of the earth'"*.

Jesus attacks their attempt at casting doubt in the minds of the people by using the story of Jonah. Just as Jonah came out of a place of certain death – the belly of a whale – so Jesus would come out of the tomb of death after three days. Did that dispel their doubts? Did that dispel their questions? Well, it may have with some people because after Jesus said these things, the crowds got bigger and bigger. But the Pharisees continued to doubt and attack. So, let me ask you this question – and answer it honestly – have you ever had doubts?

## Levels of Doubts

Have you ever dealt with doubts in your life? There are different levels of doubt. First, there are doubts that really don't make a difference. There is a card game called "I Doubt It." The object of the game is to tell what cards you have in your hand you are about to lay down, and the other players have a chance to "doubt it." The outcome of the game will not impact the direction of your life. There are other times you might doubt the information shared with you. I received a card in the mail the other day telling me I had a computer tablet waiting for me, and all I had to do was go down to the sales place and pick it up – I doubted it.

Second, there are doubts that are justified. If someone challenged you to swim across the Mississippi River and you knew you weren't a strong swimmer – your doubt would be justified. If you are not feeling well and someone says that all you have to do is "drink this green stuff," your doubts would be justified.

Could you go on one of those reality shows and not get kicked off the island? Could you accomplish the goal of learning a new language in three weeks? Could you sing a solo without scaring people away? Doubting is a part of human nature. It has been around for a long time and will continue to be around.

How do you handle doubt? Do you dismiss it? Do you see it as a challenge? Do you let it scare you to death and paralyze you from doing anything? Does it cause you just to give up and forget about what you are struggling with? In the first 18 verses of John chapter 20, we have the very familiar story – the story of Mary Magdalene coming and finding the tomb empty on that first Easter morning. Peter and another disciple joined her. Mary then has a conversation with Jesus and goes back to tell everyone what she has seen. But I am not going to dwell on that part of the chapter – I want us to see what happened after that.

I don't know if you have experienced it or not, but I have been told by those who have lost a loved one, especially a spouse, that after the funeral is over and everyone has gone home, it's the quiet moments, when you are all alone, that are the roughest. The haunting question of "What do I do now?" fills the room. That describes the scene we are going to read.

Let's pick up the story in John 20:19: *"That Sunday evening the disciples were meeting behind locked doors because they were afraid of the Jewish leaders."* But the scene quickly changed: *"Suddenly, Jesus was standing there among them! 'Peace be with you,' he said. As he spoke, he showed them the wounds in his hands and his side. They were filled with joy when they saw the Lord! Again he said, 'Peace be with you. As the Father has sent me, so I am sending you.' Then he breathed on them and said, 'Receive the Holy Spirit. If you forgive anyone's sins, they are forgiven. If you do not forgive them, they are not forgiven.' One of the disciples, Thomas (nicknamed the Twin), was not with the others when Jesus came. They told him, 'We have seen the Lord!' But he replied, 'I won't believe it unless I see the nail wounds in his hands, put my fingers into them, and place my hand into the wound in his side'"* (John 20:19-25).

Do you get the picture? The disciples were afraid, not sure what to do. There was so much excitement that morning, and now everything was quiet. They locked the door, looked at each other, and asked, "What do we do now?" Jesus answered their question when He broke into their world and renewed their hope. They were all filled with joy, all but one. Thomas. He wasn't buying it: *"Eight days later the disciples were together again, and this time Thomas was with them. The doors were locked; but suddenly, as before, Jesus was standing among them. 'Peace be with you,' he said. Then he said to Thomas, 'Put your finger here, and look at my hands. Put your hand into the wound in my side. Don't be faithless any longer. Believe!' 'My Lord and my God!' Thomas exclaimed. Then Jesus told him, 'You believe because you have seen me. Blessed are those who believe without seeing me.' The disciples saw Jesus do many other miraculous signs in addition to the ones recorded in this book. But these are written so that you may continue to believe that Jesus is the Messiah, the Son of God, and that by believing in him you will have life by the power of his name"* (John 20:26-31).

Jesus knew that those who believed in Him would be challenged. That includes even you and me. If we are honest with ourselves, there have probably been times in our lives when we had some doubts. Is Jesus really who He said He was? If God is so good, why does so much bad happen? How am I supposed to trust in God for my future when I am having a hard time just getting through today?

When doubt creeps in, we can find hope in the events of John 20. Let me share with you four things I think we can learn from this chapter about doubt and hope—hope that comes because of the resurrection.

### When Doubts Creep In: Seek Out Those Who Have the Hope of Jesus

John 20:19 says, *"That Sunday evening the disciples were meeting behind locked doors because they were afraid of the Jewish leaders."* The disciples hung together. They were scared and they were hiding, but they stayed close to each other. When Jesus appeared, they all shared that hope together.

It would have been interesting to know what they were talking about. Were they making plans for the future? Were they trying to decide what to do if the Jewish leaders found them? Were they talking about what happened in the garden, the trial, the crucifixion? I think they may have touched on all of those subjects. Most importantly, at that time, I believe they found strength in being together and having a shared hope.

When you are going through rough times in your life and not sure what to do, even to the point of doubting your faith – don't run away from the church and fellow believers – run towards them and surround yourself with them. There is value in the fellowship of believers. There is something about sharing a tough time in life that creates a special bond. If you are the one someone comes running to, let them in.

Chuck Swindoll, in his book, "Dropping Your Guard" shared an illustration I have never forgot. He said that the church needs to be like a hospital where people can come and find healing rather than a elaborate sanctuary where people come to gather to worship. The church needs to be a "one another" place that dispenses the hope of Jesus to those who need it: *"Therefore encourage one another and build each other up, just as in fact you are doing"* (1 Thessalonians 5:11); *"But encourage one another daily, as long as it is called Today"* (Hebrews 3:13).

### When Doubts Creep In: Place Your Hope in the Resurrection

Look again at what Jesus did for the disciples and Thomas. To the disciples: *"As he spoke, he showed them the wounds in his hands and his side. . ."*

." To Thomas: *"Put your finger here, and look at my hands. Put your hand into the wound in my side."* Were the disciples in shock? Were they having trouble believing what was going on? I think so. The point: Jesus gave them all the evidence needed to prove that it was really Him. They had seen him do many amazing things, but coming back to life was at the top of the chart – it was hard to grasp.

In times of doubt, we all need to objectively step back and examine the evidence. Dr. Benjamin Gilbert-West and Lord Littleton were professors at Cambridge University. They were so fed up with Christianity that they wanted to destroy it. So, they took a leave of absence to study and write a book to refute both the resurrection and the conversion of Saul of Tarsus. As a result of their study, they became ardent believers.

Dr. Simon Greenleaf was a skeptic from Harvard Law School. He had written three volumes on the law. In his classes, he mocked any Christian that was there. One day he was challenged by Christian students to apply his own book to the resurrection of Jesus. So, he took up the challenge and found the evidence to be convincing, so he became a believer.

## When Doubts Creep In: Find Your Purpose in Jesus

I love these words from Jesus to His disciples: *"As the Father has sent me, so I am sending you."* *(John 20:21).* Jesus knew just what they needed to hear. He found his disciples huddled in a room behind locked doors, afraid to go outside because the Jews might want to do the same thing to them that they did to Jesus.

What does He do? He reminds them of their purpose—"I am sending you." He empowers them by giving them the Holy Spirit. He motivates them by telling them they can forgive sins. He renews their hope through the purpose He had for them.

There have been times in ministry when I have needed to step back and say, "Wait a minute, the ministry is not all about reports, strategic plans, marketing, fund-raising, and meetings. It is about people. It's about taking care of the "least of these." It's about listening and praying for and with others. It's about sharing my story with others. Because of the resurrection, we have hope for tomorrow. Rediscover your purpose in Christ. He is sending you out on a mission – to be the hands, feet, and heart of Jesus.

## When Doubts Creep In: Trust in God's Promises

*"'Blessed are those who believe without seeing me.' . . . that by believing in him you will have life by the power of his name." (John 20:29,31)*

In the last century, there was a very prominent British philosopher named Bertrand Russell who had an interesting view of life and death. After much study, he came to the conclusion that the human experience is marked by hopelessness because of all the challenges we face in our world.

What could have prompted Bertrand Russell to write such a thing? Well, Bertrand Russell didn't believe in Jesus. He was an atheist! He rejected God and denied the resurrection of Jesus Christ. He had no hope because he did not have Jesus. The resurrection makes all the difference.

You can stop by Mohammed's grave - he is there. You can visit Confucius' grave – he is there. You can go to the grave of Buddha – he is there. No matter what world religion you might think of - their founders are all lying in the tomb... returning to dust.

You can stop by the tomb of Jesus – and guess what – nobody is home - He is not there; He is risen! Find hope in the promises of God. When you do, you will be blessed: *"You believe because you have seen me. Blessed are those who believe without seeing me"* (John 20:29). When you do, you will "have life": *"by believing in him you will have life by the power of his name"* (John 20:31).

## Study Guide: Overcoming Doubt

Pray for God's guidance and insight as you study His Word. He knows your heart and what you need to learn.

### Focus Your Mind and Heart

What do you think of when you think of the story of Jonah?

What are some doubts you have had to deal with in your life?

### Examine the Word

Take a few moments and look through the short story of Jonah. What doubts do you think Jonah may have been dealing with?

What point was Jesus trying to get the Pharisees to understand by using the story of Jonah in His response to them? (Matthew 12:38-41).

In John 20:19-31, the image of the disciple named Thomas is forever changed - he became known as "Doubting Thomas." Do you think that Thomas was the only disciple that had doubts? What could have been some of the things the disciples were doubting at that time in their lives?

### Take a Look at Your Life

When you have doubts, who do you turn to for help?

How can the resurrection of Jesus help dispel the doubts you deal with?

What difference could finding a new purpose make in dealing with doubts?

What are some of your "go-to" verses in the Bible that give you strength when you have times of doubt?

### Apply it to Your Life

Don't be afraid to admit your doubts. That is the first step in dealing with them.

Look back through John 20:19-31 and write down the things that can help you deal with the doubts you might be struggling with.

Formulate a simple prayer that you can use when you feel doubts creeping in.

# CHAPTER ELEVEN

## *Surviving Wilderness Temptations*

### Crossing the Red Sea, the Wilderness Wanderings,
### and Standing Firm in Temptation
### 1 Corinthians 10:1-13

Wouldn't it be nice if once we had victory over a temptation, we would never have to deal with it again? But you and I know that is not how it works. Temptation is a part of life, and how we deal with the temptations we face will make a big difference in our lives. I want to begin this chapter with a New Testament verse that gives us some hope when it comes to temptation.

*"No temptation has seized you except what is common to man. And God is faithful; he will not let you be tempted beyond what you can bear. But when you are tempted, he will also provide a way out so that you can stand up under it" (1 Corinthians 10:13).*

I have quoted this verse, memorized it, and referred to it several times, but I had never looked at the context of the verse until this study. What I found is that this verse is given in the context of several Old Testament stories. How do those Old Testament stories connect with dealing with temptation? I'm glad you asked.

Here's the Big Picture Context – Paul is answering a question the early Christians at Corinth had asked him about eating food sacrificed to idols. That may seem like a silly question to us, but It was a big deal in the early church because of two things: 1) Some of the trade guilds, or unions, would hold big feasts which included sacrificing animals to the pagan gods and then they would prepare the meal and serve them at their feasts; 2) The second thing was if the meat weren't served at a feast it would be taken to the market and sold. Christians were buying that meat and eating it.

The big question arose – is it right for Christians to eat meat from animals sacrificed to pagan gods? Paul addresses the question in Chapters 8-10 of 1 Corinthians. His basic answer is this – what you eat or drink is not as important as the strength of your relationship with God. What is important is how you deal with the temptations the world and culture throw at you. We can be dragged down by giving in to the culture around us – just as some of the early Christians were with some of the pagan practices.

## Don't Let the Temptations and Culture of this World Bring You Down

In 1 Corinthians 10, Paul uses Old Testament stories to teach us how to live in this world of temptation.

*"For I do not want you to be ignorant of the fact, brothers, that our forefathers were all under the cloud and that they all passed through the sea. They were all baptized into Moses in the cloud and in the sea. They all ate the same spiritual food and drank the same spiritual drink; for they drank from the spiritual rock that accompanied them, and that rock was Christ" (1 Corinthians 10:1-3).*

Paul is asking them to draw on the stories they had heard about the time that the Children of Israel were led out of Egypt after 400 years of slavery. The first comes from a well-known story – the crossing of the Red Sea. *"Then the angel of God, who had been traveling in front of Israel's army, withdrew and went behind them. The pillar of cloud also moved from in front and stood behind them, coming between the armies of Egypt and Israel. Throughout the night the cloud brought darkness to the one side and light to the other side; so neither went near the other all night long" (Exodus 14:19-22).*

Paul says they were "baptized" by the cloud and the sea. The word for baptism literally means "immersed in." That is why we baptize by immersion. Paul is reminding us that God delivered His people from their bondage of slavery and took care of them in the wilderness. He gave them manna from heaven and water from a rock. Paul says that God's spiritual hand was in all of it and over all of it. God's Spirit watched over them.

Then he goes on to say this: *"Nevertheless, God was not pleased with most of them; their bodies were scattered over the desert" (1 Corinthians 10:5).* The people didn't believe that God would deliver them into the promised land. Paul is referring to the story of 12 spies sent by Moses to check out the land (Numbers 13-14). Ten of them said the people were too weak to conquer the land. The people believed them, and God condemned them to die in the wilderness. But not everyone was on the side of the ten spies. There were two other spies who believed that they could conquer the land with the help of God. Those two men, Joshua and Caleb, were told by God that they would see the promised land.

Paul goes on to give the reason for referring to this story: *"Now these things occurred as examples to keep us from setting our hearts on evil things as they did" (1 Corinthians 10:6)*. Paul goes on then to give examples of the evil things they did. He is basically saying, "Learn from their mistakes and don't do the same things!" He gives four specific examples from the people in the wilderness:

Example 1 – *"Do not be idolaters, as some of them were; as it is written: 'The people sat down to eat and drink and got up to indulge in pagan revelry'" (1 Corinthians 10:7)*. While Moses was up on the mountain getting the ten commandments from God, the people got impatient and created a golden calf idol and basically had a big sinful party. *"So the next day the people rose early and sacrificed burnt offerings and presented fellowship offerings. Afterward they sat down to eat and drink and got up to indulge in revelry" (Exodus 32:6)*. What was the problem? The people turned to idols rather than worshipping the true God.

Example 2 - *"We should not commit sexual immorality, as some of them did — and in one day twenty-three thousand of them died" (1 Corinthians 10:8)*. Paul gives another example from Numbers 25:1-3 that applies to his message: *"While Israel was staying in Shittim, the men began to indulge in sexual immorality with Moabite women, who invited them to the sacrifices to their gods. The people ate and bowed down before these gods. So Israel joined in worshiping the Baal of Peor. And the Lord's anger burned against them."* The chapter goes on to share how God sent a plague on the people of Israel and over 23,000 people died from the plague. It did not stop until Phineas, the priest, put to death an Israelite man who had brought a Moabite woman into his home in the sight of all the people.

Example 3 – *"We should not test the Lord, as some of them did — and were killed by snakes" (1 Corinthians 10:9)*. The story Paul is referring to is found in Numbers 21:4-6: *"They traveled from Mount Hor along the route to the Red Sea, to go around Edom. But the people grew impatient on the way; they spoke against God and against Moses, and said, 'Why have you brought us up out of Egypt to die in the desert? There is no bread! There is no water! And we detest this miserable food!' Then the Lord sent venomous snakes among them; they bit the people and many Israelites died."* That is certainly a vivid example, especially for those who do not like snakes!

Example 4 – *"And do not grumble, as some of them did — and were killed by the destroying angel" (1 Corinthians 10:10).* Paul is reminding them of the events that occurred in Numbers 11:1 & 14:2: *"Now the people complained about their hardships in the hearing of the Lord, and when he heard them his anger was aroused. . .. All the Israelites grumbled against Moses and Aaron, and the whole assembly said to them, 'If only we had died in Egypt! Or in this desert!'"* The destroying angel is not specifically mentioned in Numbers, but Paul seems to be saying that the death angel we read of in Exodus with the Passover night also executes God's judgment on the people in the wilderness.

What does the New Testament do with a lot of the Old Testament stories? It uses them as examples for us to learn from. Paul says that in the next verse in our text: *"These things happened to them as examples and were written down as warnings for us, on whom the fulfillment of the ages has come" (1 Corinthians 10:11).*

All that builds up to a strong point of application for them and us: Don't be like the Children of Israel, don't let those types of things destroy our relationship with God. The Children of Israel gave into the temptations of this world rather than put their trust in God. They gave into the temptations of sexual immorality, and it led to destruction on several levels. They gave into the temptations of blaming God and grumbling against Him. They did all this while at the same time they were proclaiming that they were God's chosen people!

Paul drives home his point of application and brings us back to the verse we started with: *"So, if you think you are standing firm, be careful that you don't fall! No temptation has seized you except what is common to man. And God is faithful; he will not let you be tempted beyond what you can bear. But when you are tempted, he will also provide a way out so that you can stand up under it" (1 Corinthians 10:12,13).*

We are all in a spiritual wilderness when it comes to temptation. It is out there and can come from anywhere. If we are not prepared, the wilderness can get the best of us. Here are some spiritual survival guidelines to help us overcome the wilderness temptations we face.

### Don't Let Spiritual Pride Bring You Down

*"So, if you think you are standing firm, be careful that you don't fall"* (1 Corinthians 10:12)!

The Children of Israel, especially in Jesus' day, said, "Nothing can touch us; we are God's chosen people. We have Abraham as our father." Paul wants us to learn from what happened to them. They were not invincible, and neither are we. The moment that we let our guard down, Satan is ready to attack.

### Know that You are Not Alone

*"No temptation has seized you except what is common to man. And God is faithful; he will not let you be tempted beyond what you can bear"* (1 Corinthians 10:13a).

First, you are not alone in your temptation. Everyone deals with temptation. You are not an exception. In fact, in the second half of the verse, he doesn't say "if"; he says "when." You think you are the only one who has ever dealt with a temptation like the one you are dealing with – guess what – you're wrong. The basic temptations people deal with have been the same from the beginning of time. The good news is that there is probably someone you can seek help from who has gone through it before.

Second, God is faithful. He is there for you. *"He will not let you be tempted beyond what you can bear"* (1 Corinthians 10:13b). God knows you better than you know yourself. He has confidence in you. The rest of the verse tells us how that practically works itself out.

### There is a Way to Overcome Temptation

*"But when you are tempted, he will also provide a way out so that you can stand up under it."* (1 Corinthians 10:13c).

How do you think Moses felt when he was standing on the shore of the Red Sea with the Egyptian army bearing down on them with all their might and fury? He probably thought there was no way out.

Guess what – on his own power, there was no way out. Guess what else – with God's power, there was a way out. The same God that was on the bank of the Red Sea with Moses is the same God who is with us today. The verse says He will provide a way.

### Say "No" and Run the Other Way

Let me show you the "way out" from scripture. Say "no" and run the other way. Follow the example of Joseph in the Old Testament. When tempted by Potiphar's wife, he literally ran out of the room so fast that he had his robe ripped off of him, and he left it behind. When tempted, he ran the other way. The way to overcome temptation is to say "No." It may be running the other way – not going to that place that you know will bring you down.

### Use Scripture Like Jesus Did

When Jesus was approached by Satan in the wilderness, He used scripture to defeat the temptations of Satan. When Jesus was tempted with the weakness of the flesh – He had not eaten for 40 days – He came back with this: *"It is written: 'Man shall not live on bread alone, but on every word that comes from the mouth of God'" (Matthew 4:4)*. When tempted in the area of pride He responded: *"It is also written: 'Do not put the Lord your God to the test'" (Matthew 4:7)*. When tempted with power and authority on earth, Jesus rebuked Satan: *"Away from me, Satan! For it is written: 'Worship the Lord your God, and serve him only'" (Matthew 4:10)*.

We may not face the exact temptations Jesus did, but we face the same areas of temptation that He faced. We need to know that the way to face temptation is not to face it with our own power. The Word of God is the source of strength and the best to have ready when facing temptation.

### Pray the Prayer of David

*"Create in me a pure heart, O God, and renew a steadfast spirit within me. Do not cast me from your presence or take your Holy Spirit from me. Restore to me the joy of your salvation and grant me a willing spirit, to sustain me" (Psalm 51:10-12)*.

Sometimes, people treat the symptoms of temptation rather than the source. We can change the external circumstances of temptation – avoid that place where you are weak – avoid the people that bring you down – avoid opening the item that leads you to sin. We can do all those things, but if we don't start with the heart, we will never completely overcome the temptations before us. David's prayer is powerful. When we allow God to create a new heart in us, it takes care of the desires that many times lead us into temptation.

There is a story told of Albert Einstein on a train. The conductor came by to collect the tickets, and Albert Einstein could not find his ticket. He looked everywhere. He searched all his pockets and papers, but he could not find it. The conductor assured him that he knew who he was and that it would be fine. The Conductor went on his way down the train and then turned back to see Mr. Einstein still frantically looking for his ticket under his seat. He went back to him and assured him again that he believed him when he said he had a ticket. Mr. Einstein looked at him and reportedly said something to the effect of, "That's not the problem. I don't know where I'm going!"

Let me ask you this: when you find yourself in the wilderness of life with temptations all around you, do you know where you're going? Do you know how you're going to deal with the things that come up in your path? Paul wants to prepare us for the wilderness. He doesn't want us to find ourselves in the same mess that the children of Israel found themselves in. Let me challenge you to memorize this verse and take it to heart. When you do, you will be better equipped to face the temptations that will come your way.

*"No temptation has seized you except what is common to man. And God is faithful: he will not let you be tempted beyond what you can bear. But when you are attempted, you will also provide a way out so that you can stand up" (1 Corinthians 10:13).*

**Study Guide: Surviving Wilderness Temptations**

Pray for God's guidance and insight as you study His Word. He knows your heart and what you need to learn.

### Focus Your Mind and Heart

You may or may not remember a comedian named Flip Wilson. One of the well-known lines in his comedy was, "The devil made me do it!" It would always get a laugh, but it was not necessarily good theology. What is wrong with the line, "The devil made me do it?"

The title of this chapter was, "Surviving Wilderness Temptations." What did you think of when you first read that title?

What are some things that influence us when we deal with temptation?

### Examine the Word

We don't have the issue of eating food sacrificed to idols that Paul deals with in 1 Corinthians 8 – 10, but what are some issues we deal with today that might be similar?

What were some of the lessons that Paul wanted the Corinthians and us to learn from the past?

- 1 Corinthians 10:7 –
- 1 Corinthians 10:8 –
- 1 Corinthians 10:9 –
- 1 Corinthians 10:10 –

*"So, if you think you are standing firm, be careful that you don't fall!"* (1 Corinthians 10:12)

What are some things that could make you think you are standing firm when you really aren't?

Paul says in 1 Corinthians 10:13 that God will provide a way out when you are tempted. He doesn't give any specifics. What do you think are some of the "ways out?"

What are some of the key elements in the prayer of David in Psalm 51:10-12?

**Take a Look at Your Life**

Be honest with yourself, what are some of the toughest temptations you deal with?

How can you deal with "spiritual pride" when it tries to drag you down?

What comfort is there in knowing that you are not the only one that has faced temptation?

What are some things that you rely on to help you overcome temptation?

**Apply it to Your Life**

Look again at 1 Corinthians 10:13. Re-write it in your own words and personalize it to your life.

Memorize 1 Corinthians 10:13 and keep it ready to use when you are faced with temptation.

Revisit the temptation of Jesus in Matthew 4. Identify some ways that you can deal with temptation by seeing how Jesus dealt with temptation.

# CHAPTER TWELVE

## *Finding a Relationship with God*

### Numbers 21 & John 3

Have you ever seen the medical symbol before? It is a vertical rod with wings at the top and two serpents wound around the rod. It is known as the Caduceus. Many say it comes from the ancient Greek god of medicine – Asclepius. But others say the origin goes back much further, all the way back to the time of Moses.

I don't know if the image was carried through history and adopted by the Greeks or not, but the image of a snake on a stick, used for healing, comes from an interesting story in the Old Testament. What is even more interesting is that the Old Testament story I am referring to is found in the context of one of the most well-known verses in the Bible. Both passages—the Old Testament and New Testament—basically center on our relationship with God. I want us to think about that relationship. How is it going? Could it be better? Are there things that are keeping it from being all it could be?

### The Old Testament Story Broken Down

Numbers 21:4 starts with *"They."* Who are "they?" This is a reference to the children of Israel. They had been wandering in the wilderness in the northern part of the Sinai Peninsula—east of Egypt —for almost 40 years. What happens in this text is near the end of that 40 years of wandering.

*"They traveled from Mount Hor along the route to the Red Sea, to go around Edom. But the people grew impatient on the way; they spoke against God and against Moses, and said, 'Why have you brought us up out of Egypt to die in the desert? There is no bread! There is no water! And we detest this miserable food!'" (Number 21:4,5).*

How many of you like eating the same food day after day? When I was a youth minister several years ago, I was part of the Christ In Youth team that went to the Dominican Republic to lead a Youth Conference. We had the same food at each meal every day for a week. I can still remember it. Breakfast was a boiled egg, a piece of cheese, and fried plantains. Lunch was brown beans and rice. Supper was a piece of salami meat, boiled Yuca roots with broth gravy.

Eating the same thing for almost 40 years? I probably would have been in the middle of the mob or even leading the mob when it came to complaining about the food. But God was not amused with their behavior. Here is what happened: *"Then the Lord sent venomous snakes among them; they bit the people and many Israelites died" (Numbers 21:6).* That got their attention. They realized what they were doing and seemed to repent of their actions:

*"The people came to Moses and said, 'We sinned when we spoke against the Lord and against you. Pray that the Lord will take the snakes away from us.' So Moses prayed for the people" (Numbers 21:7).*

Their request seemed logical – get rid of the snakes. That's probably what most of us would have requested. God heard their prayer but answered it differently than what they requested.

*"The Lord said to Moses, 'Make a snake and put it up on a pole; anyone who is bitten can look at it and live.' So Moses made a bronze snake and put it up on a pole. Then when anyone was bitten by a snake and looked at the bronze snake, he lived" (Numbers 21:8,9).* So, when I first read this story, I said, "That is kind of weird." Not that the snakes came and bit the people as a punishment from God – as intriguing as that is - that is not what caught my attention. Verse 8 is what perplexed me: *"The Lord said to Moses, 'Make a snake and put it up on a pole; anyone who is bitten can look at it and live.'"*

I thought, "Isn't that kind of like creating an idol? Make a bronze snake, put it on a pole, and hold it up so that the people who look at it will not die from the snake bite. God was definitely against them having idols. So, what is all this about? That is where the "Old Made New" comes in.

## The Numbers 21 Story is Linked with One of the Best-Known Verses of the Bible – John 3:16.

John 3:16 is part of a conversation that the Pharisee Nicodemus had with Jesus. He comes to Him at night; some think this is because he doesn't want anyone to see him going to Jesus and talking to Him. Most of the Pharisees despised Jesus because He threatened their religious authority in the eyes of the people.

Nicodemus basically says to Jesus – "You are a great teacher, blessed by God. It appears that God is really with you". Jesus tells him that *"no one can see the Kingdom of God unless he is born again" (John 3:3).* Nicodemus seems to ignore Jesus' jab. As a Pharisee, Nicodemus would have felt he knew everything there was to know about the kingdom of God.

Nicodemus instead focuses on the "born again" idea. He wants to know how someone could be born again. He was seeing things from a physical perspective. Jesus was sharing insight from a spiritual perspective. Jesus keyed in on a relationship with God, not just "head knowledge." Jesus says this: *"Just as Moses lifted up the snake in the desert, so the Son of Man must be lifted up, that everyone who believes in him may have eternal life. 'For God so loved the world that he gave his one and only Son, that whoever believes in him shall not perish but have eternal life'" (John3:14-16).*

Jesus makes a direct connection between Moses' serpent—the people were healed—and His own saving work. So, I want to look at the Old Testament story and see how Jesus makes it new. We can learn at least three lessons from these two passages.

## A Relationship with God Begins with the Realization of Sin

When we think of sin, we might think of things like murder, stealing, sexual immorality, etc. But listen to what the people in the wilderness in the Old Testament said: *"We sinned when we spoke against the Lord and against you" (Numbers 21:7).* Their sin was a grumbling discontent. They did not have a relationship with God that brought contentment and thankfulness.

In the Old Testament, God graciously provided, but the people were never satisfied. In the New Testament, Nicodemus comes as a Pharisee. The Pharisees were always opposed to Jesus and were never satisfied with what He did or said.

Grumbling is just an example of something that might be building a wall between you and God. The issue is a relationship issue. Is there some sin in your life that you need to be honest about? Is there something that is blocking an open and honest relationship with God? The Israelites came clean and said, *"We sinned when we spoke against the Lord and against you" (Numbers 21:7).* We need to take sin seriously in our lives. God took it seriously in the OT and Jesus took it seriously in the New Testament.

What can be done about sin? It can be seen in the Old Testament story as well as the New Testament.

A Relationship with God Offers Healing After Repentance

Moses wasn't told to make that bronze serpent until the people had repented, and then he went to the Lord in prayer. Once they recognized the real problem—their sin—they were ready to find a solution. They asked him to pray that the snakes be taken away. The text says that Moses prayed for the people. God's answer came as a result of their realization that they had dishonored God.

Imagine being part of a team of leaders during this situation. You are tasked with solving the snake problem. The first thing you'd do is figure out a way to get rid of the snakes. Then you'd look for a salve or something to heal the wounded. Snake removal and proper medical treatment would be the focus of your efforts. Building something that looks like a snake and staring at it would probably never come up in a brainstorming session.

The Israelites were called upon to do something unusual – look at a bronze snake on a stick. The verb translated as "look" often carries with it the idea "to see with belief or understanding." God was calling on them to believe again in Him and trust what He had to say.

Many times in the Old Testament, God asks people to do things that don't make common sense. Moses – you want to cross the Red Sea? Hold your staff out over it. Gideon – you want to defeat the Midianite army of hundreds of thousands of soldiers. Arm your army of 350 men with a candle, a pitcher to cover it, and a trumpet.

In Numbers 21, God answered the prayer with a different solution than what the people had come up with. If you had asked the people in Jesus' day what they would need to do to be forgiven of their sins and go to heaven – they would have rattled off a whole bunch of things. They would list things like making the right sacrifices, obeying all the commandments of God, participating in all the religious festivals, etc. The Pharisees had done a good job of teaching them the checklist they needed to follow.

What did Jesus say to Nicodemus about what it took to be born again? *"Just as Moses lifted up the snake in the desert, so the Son of Man must be lifted up, that everyone who believes in him may have eternal life"* (John 3:14,15). Why didn't God just take away the snakes like they asked? I wonder if He left the snakes as a reminder to them that they needed to trust in Him and not themselves. Why doesn't God just take away all the sins in the world? Because it is the reality of our sins that should bring us to our knees and turn to the one who died for our sins.

## A Relationship with God is Founded in Love

Have you ever gone to the doctor when you were sick? Probably. Some of you pride yourself on never going to the doctor, but there are times when you need to. Going to the doctor is an admission that you need help and you can't take care of this yourself.

Likewise, we need to go to God to experience His love and mercy. Unless we are people of repentance, we will never be able to receive God's mercy and grow in our relationship with Him. *"For God so loved the world that he gave his one and only Son, that whoever believes in him shall not perish but have eternal life. For God did not send his Son into the world to condemn the world, but to save the world through him"* (John 3:16,17).

When you see judgment in the pages of the Bible – snakes come and begin biting people and they die - look deeper at what is going on. There are two sides to the coin. When we flip the judgment coin over, we see that God's amazing love and mercy are on the other side. Because He is holy, He must deal with our sins. Because He is love, He sent His one and only son to die for our sins.

It basically all comes down to this. Are you willing to look up to the one who was lifted on that stick called a cross to find the healing that only God can give?

## Study Guide: Finding A Relationship with God

Pray for God's guidance and insight as you study His Word. He knows your heart and what you need to learn.

### Focus Your Mind and Heart

When a problem comes up and you have to find a solution, what are some of the steps involved in solving the problem?

Do you know anyone who has ever sinned? If you are having trouble identifying someone, just look in the mirror!

What are some solutions for sin?

### Examine the Word

The story in Numbers 21:4-9 is not as well known as some of the other stories in the Old Testament. Can you think of some other Old Testament stories that show the unfaithfulness of the Children of Israel?

Looking at the context of a verse in the Bible is always a good component of Bible study. How does looking at the context of John 3:16 help you think about or see things that you have never thought of?

Numbers 21:7 says, "We sinned when we spoke against the Lord and against you." How important is the realization of sin in our walk with God?

What is Jesus referring to in John 3:14,15 when He says, "Just as Moses lifted up the snake in the desert, so the Son of Man must be lifted up"?

### Take a Look at Your Life

When you think of having a relationship with God, what are some of the things that get in the way?

What are some things that help you grow in your relationship with God?

**Apply it to Your Life**

Do you have some sins in your life that you need to admit to and confess them to God? If so, take some time in prayer and do that right now.

John 3:16 is probably one of the most memorized verses in the Bible. If you have memorized it, great! If not, memorize it now, only with a little twist: instead of the word "world," insert your own name.

# CHAPTER THIRTEEN

## Find What's Missing

### The Old and New Sacrifices as Seen in Hebrews 9-10

Have you ever had this happen to you? You go to finish a puzzle, and there is a missing piece. You will look on the table, under the table, in the box, on the bottom of your shoe. Why? You already know what the puzzle is a picture of. It's not as if you put the piece in and say, "Aha. I see it now. It's a picture of a mountain lake"! But it is still frustrating to have a missing piece. It is not complete until that missing piece is put in place.

We are going to look at something like that in this chapter. Something was missing in the Old Testament story. It was a very important piece because it dealt with a crucial issue—forgiveness of sin. As we continue our study of the "Old Made New," we are going to find what was missing and hopefully let that missing part fill the void we have in our own lives.

### The Old Testament System of Sacrifice was Missing Something

We will look at some passages in the New Testament book of Hebrews. Hebrews draws from the Old Testament more than any other book when it comes to making the Old Testament new. In chapter nine, we find a discussion of the covenant between God and Israel: *"That first covenant between God and Israel had regulations for worship and a place of worship here on earth. There were two rooms in that Tabernacle. In the first room were a lampstand, a table, and sacred loaves of bread on the table. This room was called the Holy Place"* (Hebrews 9:1,2 - NLT).

Verses three through five describe the major contents of this room. After giving that description, it goes on: *"When these things were all in place, the priests regularly entered the first room as they performed their religious duties. But only the high priest ever entered the Most Holy Place, and only once a year. And he always offered blood for his own sins and for the sins the people had committed in ignorance"* (Hebrews 9:6,7 - NLT). Why is this being described?

The writer of Hebrews wants us to see the contrast between the old way of doing things and the new. He goes on to say this:

*"This is an illustration pointing to the present time. For the gifts and sacrifices that the priests offer is not able to cleanse the consciences of the people who bring them. For that old system deals only with food and drink and various cleansing ceremonies—physical regulations that were in effect only until a better system could be established"* (Hebrews 9:9,10 - NLT).

At this point, it will be helpful to have a brief explanation of the Old Testament sacrificial system. As detailed and methodical as the Old Testament sacrificial system was, it never could bring complete forgiveness and cleansing of the people for whom the sacrifices were given. Once a year, the High Priest would make a sacrifice for all the people. But guess what? He would have to do it again the next year.

The book of Leviticus contains five major offerings for the people. I'm not going to go over all of them, but trust me when I say that the element that was missing was that the system never completed the process. That is what is meant in verse 10: *"For that old system deals only with food and drink and various cleansing ceremonies—physical regulations that were in effect only until a better system could be established."*

## Something Better was Coming

While attending a conference for fire chaplains in Ocala, FL, I took a tour of the "E-One" factory, which builds fire trucks. They gave the history of the factory and showed the improvement of the equipment over the years. It seemed that one question they were always asking was, "What can we do to make our fire engines better?"

The Book of Hebrews takes Old Testament teachings and basically says that Jesus made the old system better. He is what made the "old" system "new."

## Jesus is What was Missing in the Old Testament System

The whole Old Testament, every book, points toward the great sacrifice that was to come—that of Jesus' sacrificial giving of His own life on our behalf. Leviticus 17:11 is the Old Testament's central statement about the significance of blood in the sacrificial system.

God, speaking to Moses, declares: *"For the life of a creature is in the blood, and I have given it to you to make atonement for yourselves on the altar; it is the blood that makes atonement for one's life."*

In the New Testament, Jesus became the ultimate sacrifice when He died and shed His blood on the cross for your sins and mine. That is why the writer of Hebrews goes on to say in Hebrews 9:11-15:

*"So Christ has now become the High Priest over all the good things that have come. He has entered that greater, more perfect Tabernacle in heaven, which was not made by human hands and is not part of this created world. With his own blood—not the blood of goats and calves—he entered the Most Holy Place once for all time and secured our redemption forever. Under the old system, the blood of goats and bulls and the ashes of a young cow could cleanse people's bodies from ceremonial impurity. Just think how much more the blood of Christ will purify our consciences from sinful deeds so that we can worship the living God. For by the power of the eternal Spirit, Christ offered himself to God as a perfect sacrifice for our sins. That is why he is the one who mediates a new covenant between God and people, so that all who are called can receive the eternal inheritance God has promised them. For Christ died to set them free from the penalty of the sins they had committed under that first covenant"* (NLT).

Considering all of that, I want to ask you an important question—Is there anything missing in your life? Have you ever had doubts about your forgiveness? Have you ever had a time when you just couldn't find peace in your life? Have you ever struggled with your purpose in life? If you have ever dealt with any of those questions – Jesus will help you find what is missing.

The book of Hebrews shows us that Jesus made the old system obsolete and then made the whole system new on the cross. Because of that, we can go to Him to find the missing pieces in our lives.

### Jesus Provides the Missing Piece or Pieces in Our Own Lives

He offers "propitiation." When was the last time you used that word? When was the last time you wondered about your propitiation? Maybe you have never heard of it. It is a great word. It is used in the King James Version of the Bible and describes something amazing. 1 John 2:2 describes it: *"He himself is the sacrifice that atones for our sins—and not only our sins but the sins of all the world."* My definition is this: Jesus took care of the mess that sin created by dying on the cross as the perfect sacrifice.

Is forgiveness a missing piece in your life? Do you need to be forgiven of some things that have been keeping you from enjoying a saving relationship with Jesus? If so, take some time to ponder the following truths.

### He Offers Peace

We often don't have peace because we don't have answers. We just don't know what to do. We lack the confidence we need to move forward. Listen to this amazing passage in Hebrews 10 as the writer continues this train of thought that Jesus filled the missing piece:

*"And so, dear brothers and sisters, we can boldly enter heaven's Most Holy Place because of the blood of Jesus. By his death, Jesus opened a new and life-giving way through the curtain into the Most Holy Place. And since we have a great High Priest who rules over God's house, let us go right into the presence of God with sincere hearts fully trusting him. For our guilty consciences have been sprinkled with Christ's blood to make us clean, and our bodies have been washed with pure water. Let us hold tightly without wavering to the hope we affirm, for God can be trusted to keep his promise" (Hebrews 10:19-23 – NLT).*

Our peace does not lie within ourselves. Ultimately, the peace that passes understanding, as Paul describes it, is based on the fact that Jesus came and made all things new. The last phrase sums it up well: *"for God can be trusted to keep his promise."* Maybe the missing piece in your journey to find peace is trusting in the faithfulness of God's promises.

### He Offers Purpose

Life without purpose is an empty life. The world offers to fill that empty spot with all kinds of things promising fulfillment. Most of those things only fill the void temporarily or worsen the emptiness. Do you need a purpose for your life? The writer of Hebrews, after tracing the amazing story of the old and new in great theological detail, gives us very practical applications: *"Let us think of ways to motivate one another to acts of love and good works. And let us not neglect our meeting together, as some people do, but encourage one another, especially now that the day of his return is drawing near" (Hebrews 10:24-25 - NLT).*

Find purpose in thinking of ways to motivate others to acts of love and good works. When was the last time you dedicated some time to thinking about how you could help others love one another and help one another? If you and I did that more often, this world may be a better place to live.

Find purpose in worshipping together and meeting with other believers. As important as individual worship is with God, God also wants you to worship together with others. Gathering with others is powerful. It happens not only in corporate worship services but also in small groups. Much of the ministry to one another in the church happens when people in small groups share their needs and step up to meet those needs.

Find purpose in encouraging others. It is amazing the difference that takes place when you take the focus off of yourself and focus on encouraging someone else. It changes perspective. It changes attitude. It changes purpose. God knows that it is important for believers to encourage others. You can make that your newfound purpose!

What should be your motivation for all of this? Jesus is coming back. His return is drawing near. Will you be found living a life of purpose for Him?

## Study Guide: Find What's Missing

Pray for God's guidance and insight as you study His Word. He knows your heart and what you need to learn.

### Focus Your Mind and Heart

Have you ever bought something and brought it home only to find a part missing? What did you do?

What do you know about the Old Testament system of sacrifices?

What takes the place of the Old Testament sacrificial system today?

### Examine the Word

The Book of Hebrews is obviously written to an audience that had a good working knowledge of the Old Testament sacrificial system. Why would it be a challenge to write the same kind message today?

What is the main problem with the old system presented in Hebrews 9:9-10?

Leviticus 17:11 says, *"For the life of a creature is in the blood, and I have given it to you to make atonement for yourselves on the altar; it is the blood that makes atonement for one's life."* The key word in this verse is "atonement." What does "atonement" mean?

What is the contrast being made between the blood of goats and calves with the blood of Jesus in Hebrews 9:11-15?

How does 1 John 2:2, *"He himself is the sacrifice that atones for our sins—and not only our sins but the sins of all the world,"* work in concert with the Hebrews 9 passage?

Look at Hebrews 10:19-23 and list the amazing promises given because of Jesus.

### Take a Look at Your Life

How do these words from Hebrews 10:21-22 make you feel: *"And since we have a great High Priest who rules over God's house, let us go right into the presence of God with sincere hearts fully trusting him"?*

How does Jesus help you find purpose in life?

**Apply it to Your Life**

Do you have any "missing pieces" in your life that you need Jesus to fill? If so, go to Him in prayer and ask Him to fill in those empty spots in your life.

# CHAPTER FOURTEEN

## *The Old Made New at the Cross*

### Isaiah 53; Matthew 27; John 19

Have you ever gone to a computer store to buy a computer? You find the one you want with all the bells and whistles and excitedly go to the checkout counter. The salesman's first question when checking you out is, "Would you like a 2-year warranty with that?" When I hear that, I always think to myself, "If this thing won't last more than two years, should I even buy it?" It seems that you can't depend on anything to last these days.

I would like a sure thing every now and then. When you get homeowner's insurance in Florida for one year, there is no guarantee that you will be able to get it next year. When you sign up for a health care plan, you can be assured that in a year, you will have to choose a new or revised plan.

I want to propose that there is a sure thing we can depend on. That sure thing is this—God had things under control in the past, and God has things under control now. As you read through the Bible, you will find a consistent and purposeful message. There are ups and downs in the history of the Children of Israel, but through it all, God is still the God of His people. We can find assurance in knowing that God has been in control and will be in control to the very end.

This chapter wraps up our study on the "Old Made New." The purpose of the study was to help us see how the Old Testament and New Testament present one consistent message from God. Too often, people separate the two and think that they have nothing to do with each other. Nothing could be further from the truth.

For the New Testament writers, who were directed by the Holy Spirit, the Old Testament was their Bible. They would take the stories of the Old Testament and apply them to what it meant to live as a Christian in the first-century church – just as we use the New Testament to see what it means to live as a Christian today.

One of the big stories of the New Testament is the crucifixion of Jesus. When thinking of the "Old Made New," I don't think anybody would be surprised by the statement that the Old Testament predicted Christ's death on the cross. But I don't know how many of us have looked at the details, accuracy, and depth of the Old Testament prophecies concerning Christ's death. As I researched this, one thing stood out: God had things under control in the past, and God has things under control now. God, who is the same yesterday, today, and forever, is the same God you can count on now.

On the day of Jesus' resurrection, two guys were walking down the road going to the town of Emmaus. They were talking and confused about everything that they heard had happened. Suddenly a moment of clarity came. Jesus joined them, though they didn't know who He was. In the Gospel of Luke, we find that conversation, and what Jesus had to say to them: *"And beginning with Moses and all the Prophets, he explained to them what was said in all the Scriptures concerning Himself"* (Luke 24:27). Wouldn't you have loved to be in on that teaching session from Jesus!

As Jesus spoke to those men, I wonder if He zeroed in on the Scriptures that talked about the crucifixion. We can't say for sure, but I want to focus on the crucifixion of Jesus. It is important to see how God knew what was going to happen, down to the very detail, many years before it happened. He is the same God who is taking care of things today. We know the big picture. We know the story. But have you ever thought about the details, not just of the story but the accuracy of the details given 700 to 1200 years before it happened? Let's walk through the crucifixion and see the accuracy of the Old Testament prophecies and their fulfillment in the New Testament.

## The Purpose of the Crucifixion

Did the crucifixion happen because the Jewish leaders were in a bad mood and Jesus had a bad day? I don't think so. Look at these New Testament passages that explain its purpose: *"God made him who had no sin to be sin for us, so that in him we might become the righteousness of God"* (2 Corinthians 5:21); *"He himself bore our sins in his body on the tree, so that we might die to sins and live for righteousness; by his wounds you have been healed"* (1 Peter 2:24). It is clear that the purpose of the crucifixion was for us to have forgiveness for our sins.

What was said about its purpose through the prophet Isaiah some 700 years before Jesus? *"Yet it was our weaknesses he carried; it was our sorrows that weighed him down. And we thought his troubles were a punishment from God, a punishment for his own sins! But he was pierced for our rebellion, crushed for our sins. He was beaten so we could be whole. He was whipped so we could be healed"* (Isaiah 53:4,5 – NLT). Seven hundred years before it happened, the purpose was stated. God had it under control then; He's got it under control now.

### The Timing of the Crucifixion

The Old Testament story of the Passover is the foundation of the sacrifice of Christ. *"On that same night I will pass through Egypt and strike down every firstborn — both men and animals — and I will bring judgment on all the gods of Egypt. I am the Lord. The blood will be a sign for you on the houses where you are; and when I see the blood, I will pass over you. No destructive plague will touch you when I strike Egypt"* (Exodus 12:12,13).

In the New Testament the image of Christ as the Passover Lamb is repeated many times:

- *"For you know that it was not with perishable things such as silver or gold that you were redeemed from the empty way of life handed down to you from your forefathers, but with the precious blood of Christ, a lamb without blemish or defect"* (1 Peter 1:18-19)
- *"For Christ, our Passover lamb, has been sacrificed"* (1 Corinthians 5:7)
- *"Then I saw a Lamb, looking as if it had been slain, standing in the center of the throne, encircled by the four living creatures and the elders. . . . And they sang a new song: 'You are worthy to take the scroll and to open its seals, because you were slain, and with your blood you purchased men for God'"* (Rev 5:6-9).

When was Jesus crucified? It was during Passover, some 1200 after the first Passover. Coincidence? I don't think so. Christ became the sacrificial lamb. God had it under control then; He's got it under control now.

### The Words He Spoke at His Trial

*"When he was accused by the chief priests and the elders, he gave no answer.*

*Then Pilate asked him, 'Don't you hear the testimony they are bringing against you?' But Jesus made no reply, not even to a single charge — to the great amazement of the governor"* (Matthew 27:12-14).

Yet Isaiah told us 700 years before: *"He was oppressed and treated harshly, yet he never said a word. He was led like a lamb to the slaughter. And as a sheep is silent before the shearers, he did not open his mouth"*(Isaiah 53:7).

God had it under control then; He's got it under control now.

## What They Did With His Clothes was Even a Point of Prophecy

Here's what happened: *"When the soldiers had crucified Jesus, they divided his clothes among the four of them. They also took his robe, but it was seamless, woven in one piece from top to bottom. So they said, 'Rather than tearing it apart, let's throw dice for it'"* (John 19:23-24). This fulfilled the prophecy of Psalm 22:18 that says, *"They divide my garments among them and cast lots for my clothing."*

## His Treatment on the Cross

They pierced His side but did not break his legs. Why is that worth pointing out? Many times, the Romans would break the legs of those being crucified to speed up the death. When a person was nailed to a cross, they would use their legs to lift themselves up. This would ease some of the pressure on the lungs and make it easier to breathe. Here is what happened with Jesus: *"Instead, one of the soldiers pierced Jesus' side with a spear, bringing a sudden flow of blood and water. The man who saw it has given testimony, and his testimony is true. He knows that he tells the truth, and he testifies so that you also may believe. These things happened so that the scripture would be fulfilled: 'Not one of his bones will be broken'"* (John 19:34-36). The prophet Isaiah, some 700 years prior, said: *"But he was pierced for our rebellion, crushed for our sins. He was beaten so we could be whole"* (Isaiah 53:5). The Psalmist, over 1000 years before Christ writes: *"he protects all his bones, not one of them will be broken"* (Psalm 34:20). All of this also correlates with the directions given for the Passover lamb in Exodus, 1200 years before Christ. Instructions were given that none of the bones of the sacrificial lamb were to be broken.

## He was Beaten and Whipped

The details of how Jesus was treated prior to His death on the cross were prophesied. Even His treatment had a purpose. Pilate, unbeknown to him, even played a role in God's plan: *"Then he released Barabbas to them. But he had Jesus flogged, and handed him over to be crucified"* (Matthew 27:26). This detail was not overlooked in Isaiah: *"He was beaten so we could be whole. He was whipped so we could be healed"* (Isaiah 53:5). God had it under control then, He's got it under control now.

## The Very Words He Spoke on the Cross were Prophesied

*"About three in the afternoon Jesus cried out in a loud voice, 'Eli, Eli, lema sabachthani?' (which means 'My God, my God, why have you forsaken me?')"* (Matthew 27:46). When saying these words Jesus quoted from Psalm 22:1: *"My God, my God, why have you forsaken me?"*

*"Jesus called out with a loud voice, 'Father, into your hands I commit my spirit.' When he had said this, he breathed his last"* (Luke 23:46). Those words come from Psalm 31:5: *"Into your hands I commit my spirit; deliver me, Lord, my faithful God."*

*"Later, knowing that everything had now been finished, and so that Scripture would be fulfilled, Jesus said, 'I am thirsty'"* (John 19:28). This imagery comes from Psalm 22:15 and 69:21: *"My mouth is dried up like a potsherd, and my tongue sticks to the roof of my mouth; you lay me in the dust of death.";* *"They put gall in my food and gave me vinegar for my thirst."*

## Where He was Buried was Foretold

This is what Isaiah says about his burial: *"He had done no wrong and had never deceived anyone. But he was buried like a criminal; he was put in a rich man's grave"* (Isaiah 53:9). This is what happened to Jesus: *"It was Preparation Day (that is, the day before the Sabbath). So as evening approached, Joseph of Arimathea, a prominent member of the Council, who was himself waiting for the kingdom of God, went boldly to Pilate and asked for Jesus' body. . . So Joseph bought some linen cloth, took down the body, wrapped it in the linen, and placed it in a tomb cut out of rock. Then he rolled a stone against the entrance of the tomb"* (Mark 15:42, 43 46).

## What Does All This Teach Us?

In a world that can't guarantee much of anything, God had it under control then, He's got it under control now. God had a plan from the very beginning. He didn't make it up day by day. Jesus is the fulfillment of all of God's Word, the Old Testament and the New.

In a world that seems out of control, it is good to be reminded that God's got this. Throughout scripture, we can see that God has been consistent and accurate in His plan from the beginning of time and will continue to carry it out until the end of time. And the good news is this—to all those who know Him and trust in Him—He's got this.

I want to close this study by sharing the words of Isaiah 53. It is the most beautiful and prophetic passage in the Old Testament regarding Jesus's death. I referred to it several times above, but I want you to read it without any breaks or comments. As you read these words, be assured that God had it under control then, and He's Got it under control now.

## Isaiah 53

*"My servant grew up in the Lord's presence like a tender green shoot, like a root in dry ground. There was nothing beautiful or majestic about his appearance, nothing to attract us to him. He was despised and rejected—a man of sorrows, acquainted with deepest grief. We turned our backs on him and looked the other way. He was despised, and we did not care. Yet it was our weaknesses he carried; it was our sorrows that weighed him down. And we thought his troubles were a punishment from God, a punishment for his own sins! But he was pierced for our rebellion, crushed for our sins. He was beaten so we could be whole. He was whipped so we could be healed. All of us, like sheep, have strayed away. We have left God's paths to follow our own. Yet the Lord laid on him the sins of us all. He was oppressed and treated harshly, yet he never said a word. He was led like a lamb to the slaughter. And as a sheep is silent before the shearers, he did not open his mouth. Unjustly condemned, he was led away. No one cared that he died without descendants, that his life was cut short in midstream. But he was struck down for the rebellion of my people. He had done no wrong and had never deceived anyone. But he was buried like a criminal; he was put in a rich man's grave. But it was the Lord's good plan to crush him and cause him grief. Yet when his life is made an offering for sin, he will have many descendants. He will enjoy a long life, and the Lord's good plan will prosper in his hands. When he sees all that is accomplished by his anguish, he will be satisfied. And because of his experience, my righteous servant will make it possible for many to be counted righteous, for he will bear all their sins" (Isaiah 53:2-12).*

## Study Guide: The Old Made New at the Cross

Pray for God's guidance and insight as you study His Word. He knows your heart and what you need to learn.

### Focus Your Mind and Heart

What is a "sure thing" you can count on in today's world?

How would you respond to someone who says, "We don't need the Old Testament. The New Testament is all that matters"?

How does the crucifixion of Jesus fit into the story of the Bible?

### Examine the Word

What amazing truths do you find in the following verses:

2 Corinthians 5:21 –

1 Peter 2:24 -

The accuracy and consistency of the Word of God are displayed by Jesus's crucifixion. Do your own side-by-side comparison of the Old Testament passages and the New Testament fulfillment:

- The Timing – Exodus 12:12,13 and 1 Peter 1:18-19; 1 Corinthians 5:7
- His Words at Trial– Isaiah 53:7 and Matthew 27:12-14
- His Clothes – Psalm 22:18 and John 19:23-24
- His Treatment – Isaiah 53:5; Psalm 34:20 and John 19:34-36
- His Beating – Isaiah 53:5 and Matthew 27:26
- His Words on the Cross – Psalm 22:1,15; 31:5; 69:21 and Matthew 27:46; Luke 23:46; John 19:28
- His Burial – Isaiah 53:9 and Mark 15:42,43-46

### Take a Look at Your Life

How can looking at the above passages strengthen your faith?

Where would you be without the sacrifice of Jesus on the cross?

**Apply it to Your Life**

Read through Isaiah 53 again. Underline the passages that touch your heart. Let God amaze you once again with His plan and purpose.

## Afterword

"Wow, that took more work than I thought it would!" That pretty well sums up how I felt when I finished this book. This book is my first attempt at doing a book on my own. It is something I have thought about for many years but never attempted. My prayer is that it will be helpful to someone in some way. My prayer when I preach is always, "Lord, you know the needs of everyone here. Touch us where we need to be touched." That is my prayer for this book, also.

After writing the book, I decided to add the Study Guide at the end of each chapter. I hope that this will enhance personal and small-group study. What is shared is simply an outline with some suggested questions. The format can be used for almost any type of lesson. It is based on a plan I learned in Bible College: Hook, Book, Look, and Took!

# Bibliography & Notes

General

- Unless otherwise noted, all Scripture quotations are from THE HOLY BIBLE, NEW INTERNATIONAL VERSION®, NIV® Copyright © 1973, 1978, 1984, 2011 by Biblica, Inc.® Used by permission. All rights reserved worldwide.


Chapter 10:

- Chuck Swindoll's book *"Dropping Your Guard"* contains advice, tools, and suggestions designed to help people, particularly Christians, create long-lasting relationships. I highly recommend purchasing this book.
- History is full of people that started off as atheists but became believers after study of the Bible. The illustrations of Dr. Benjamin Gilbert-West, Lord Littleton, and Dr. Simon Greenleaf are just of few of the stories that demonstrate the power of the Gospel to change lives.
- Bertrand Russell's essay "A Free Man's Worship" is found within his book *"Mysticism and Logic"*. The book is an interesting collection of Mr. Russell's lifelong pursuit of truth in the modern world. The contrast between his philosophy and Christianity is worth reading, studying, and contemplation.


Chapter 11:

- The anecdote regarding Albert Einstein is well known and in the field of common knowledge. As we finish this book, I encourage you to continue studying God's word so that you don't forget where you are going.

www.ingramcontent.com/pod-product-compliance
Lightning Source LLC
Chambersburg PA
CBHW051539120626
46551CB00013B/1296